PRAISE FOR
THE PURPOSE-GUIDED UNIVERSE

"In his thought-provoking and easily-read book *The Purpose-Guided Universe* Haisch shows that it is indeed possible to be a scientist and a believer in God provided you have an open attitude to both science and religion. Indeed, after tackling the big questions of quantum nonlocality, consciousness, evolution and the nature of the Universe, he claims that belief in the absence of God presents more difficulties for an informed thinker than in the presence of God. Having accepted this main thrust of the book, many may not accept his particular religious stance, namely, Perennial Philosophy, but surely no religion has a monopoly on the truth as we explore common ground openly in the 21st century. Super book."

—Prof. Eric Priest, FRS, Mathematics Institute,
St. Andrews University, Scotland

"*The Purpose-Guided Universe* convinces me on the basis of hard logic that the physical laws, constants, and thermodynamic principles shaping and sustaining every aspect of the universe point to an underlying creative and ordering mind that has perennially been termed God. Bernard Haisch adds new scientific clarity and interpretive nuance to what many thoughtful physicists of our time believe—this universe is most plausibly the work of a creative presence. *The Purpose-Guided Universe* is elegantly written and can be understood by the informed lay reader, yet it is such a conceptually clear work that it should appeal widely to professional scientists in all fields. It could easily be used with immense benefit in undergraduate or graduate teaching in the sciences or humanities."

—Stephen G. Post, PhD,
Professor of Preventive Medicine and Director, Center for Medical
Humanities, Compassionate Care, and Bioethics, Stony Brook University

"*The Purpose-Guided Universe* makes the case for God, and the case for science, together. How sad (and, furthermore, how strange) it is, that making such a case should be even necessary today! The evidence for science (e.g., the evidence for Darwinian evolution) is overwhelming. The evidence for God is, if anything, even more overwhelming. Yet, our laggard secular culture militates against belief in God. The great thing about science is not that we can prove that something is correct (we cannot) it is that we can prove that something is wrong (hypotheses that are falsifiable). And we have proven that the universe has no existence apart from our own consciousnesses. Haisch also points out the extraordinary character of our universe—how, against all odds, our universe permits life (and in particular, permits us). While this second argument is less persuasive to me, given the current incomplete state of our knowledge of physics, it is nonetheless deeply interesting. So—if you want to reconcile science and religion? Well, simply buy this book!"

—Prof. Richard Conn Henry, Department of Physics and Astronomy, Johns Hopkins University

"The search for purpose is common to all people on Earth. Bernard Haisch, a world-class astrophysicist, finds purpose in the dynamics of the universe. If the universe has purpose, so does our life. Haisch asks the big question. He may not give the only possible answer, but his answers are certainly original. He equates belief in string theory solving all questions to belief in intelligence as the origin of fine-tuning. Religious experience speaks for the latter, providing a purpose for the universe: the conversion of potentiality to experience. It is a pleasure to read the direct and fast language, and the reader readily excuses some of his sweeping statements, such as on organized religion. Of particular interest is the quantum mechanical perspective, which is presented superbly and at the latest stage. Haisch is certainly not mainstream, but a refreshing wind from the West. Enjoy!"

—Prof. Arnold O. Benz, Institute of Astronomy, ETH Zurich, Switzerland

"Haisch, a well known astrophysicist, argues that religion and God should be acceptable by science when obvious misconceptions and excesses are eliminated. He agrees with recent authors such as Dawkins, Harris or Hitchins who criticize the organized religions because of their intolerance, brainwashing and unrestricted power in human society. Following the idea behind Ockham's razor (that simple explanations are often closer to the truth than complicated ones), Haisch argues that to suppose the existence of God is a much simpler idea than to accept current speculations about enormous numbers of alternate universes where only a single one exists in which the constants of nature are so fine tuned that life and intelligent life could evolve in it. Haisch argues that consciousness and free will is very likely an outcome of quantum mechanics and that there is no inconsistency in believing in Einstein, Darwin and God."

—Prof. Peter Ulmschneider, Institute for Theoretical Astrophysics, University of Heidelberg

THE
PURPOSE-GUIDED
UNIVERSE

BELIEVING IN
EINSTEIN, DARWIN,
AND GOD

BERNARD HAISCH

New Page Books
A Division of The Career Press Inc.
Franklin Lakes, N.J.

The Purpose-Guided Universe
Edited by Kate Henches
Typeset by Gina Hoogerhyde
Cover design by Wes Youssi/Tweedfiero
Printed in the U.S.A. by Courier

Figures by Marsha Sims (*www.marshasims.com*)

To order this title, please call toll-free 1-800-CAREER-1 (NJ and Canada: 201-848-0310) to order using VISA or MasterCard, or for further information on books from Career Press.

The Career Press, Inc., 3 Tice Road, PO Box 687,
Franklin Lakes, NJ 07417
www.careerpress.com
www.newpagebooks.com

Library of Congress Cataloging-in-Publication Data

Haisch, Bernard, 1949-
The purpose-guided universe : believing in Einstein, Darwin, and God / by Bernard Haisch.
    p. cm.
Includes bibliographical references and index.
ISBN 978-1-60163-122-0 — ISBN 978-1-60163-733-8 (ebook)
1. Religion and science. 2. God. 3. Teleology. I. Title.
    BL240.3.H355 2010
    215—dc22

                                                    2010008938

ACKNOWLEDGMENTS

This book is dedicated to my wife and best friend, Marsha Sims, and to my children, Kate, Taylor, and Elizabeth. Also to Pamela Eakins, Joyce Eakins, Jason Brenneman, and especially little James West Brenneman.

Marsha also deserves thanks for producing figures that clarify difficult but essential concepts.

I also thank Patrick Huyghe, whose contributions to *The God Theory* significantly helped its success and thereby led to the present book.

I acknowledge the classical education I received at the Latin School of Indianapolis, which in its own way wound up leading me to this book. And thanks, LSI classmates.

CONTENTS

PREFACE
9

INTRODUCTION
15

1 *SCIENCE AND RELIGION*
31

2 *QUANTUM REALITY*
47

3 *THE FINELY TUNED UNIVERSE*
67

4 *The Perennial Philosophy*
87

5 *Thou Art That*
105

6 *The God Theory*
119

7 *Staying Out of Heaven*
135

8 *Consciousness and Reality*
151

9 *The Post-Physics Era*
169

10 *The Primacy of Consciousness*
181

11 *Where Do Things Stand?*
193

Bibliography
209

Index
213

About the Author
221

PREFACE

Is it possible that there is a purpose behind the universe? One that is consistent with modern science and especially the Big Bang and evolution? I propose that there is such a grand purpose and that this has profound implications for the meaning of our lives.

More than 30 years ago, Nobel laureate Steven Weinberg famously (some would say infamously) wrote in his book, *The First Three Minutes*: "The more the universe seems comprehensible, the more it also seems pointless." This is a pretty bleak view of things. If the universe is pointless, then probably so are we. That is not a life-enhancing perspective. There is no joy in Mudville.

Things have changed dramatically since then. The evidence today is quite the opposite. It has come to light in the fields of physics and astrophysics over the past two decades that there are numerous coincidences and fine-tunings of the laws of nature that altogether seem extraordinarily unlikely and need to be explained. These key properties of the Universe have just the right values to make life possible. These are discussed in Chapter 3.

To be fair, it is possible to explain these coincidences and fine-tunings as just a matter of statistics. This involves a concept called the multiverse. The concept of the multiverse is that our apparently special universe is just one of a vast number of universes, all of which may be different from each other in unimaginable ways. There is no evidence whatsoever for this, but it makes for an interesting theory.

I am proposing that an equally likely—and perhaps even slightly more likely—explanation is that there is a conscious intelligence behind the universe, and that the purpose of the universe and of our human lives is very intimately involved with that intelligence.

The intelligence I am proposing—and we might as well call it God—has nothing to do with the anti-evolutionary view called "intelligent design." On the contrary, a Big Bang 13.7 billion years ago, a 4.6 billion-year-old Earth, and Darwinian evolution are essential ingredients of a purposeful universe in the view I present. This God needs Darwin to carry out his plan.

Two of the most prominent and accomplished astrophysicists of the last century were Sir James Jeans and Sir Arthur Eddington. Both espoused the view that consciousness was likely the foundation of the universe itself. Jeans wrote in his *The Mysterious Universe*: "The universe begins to look more like a great thought than like a great machine." Even Max Planck, the discoverer of the quantum, wrote in *The Universe in Light of Modern Physics* that "there are realities existing apart from our sense perceptions." And exceptional human experiences and accounts of mystics throughout the ages point in the same direction of a fundamental underlying consciousness. There is indeed mounting evidence from the opposite side of physics—the microscopic realm of quantum mechanics—that this view of consciousness as the basis of reality is correct.

As long ago as 1932, mathematician John von Neumann showed that quantum mechanics requires consciousness to produce any kind of measurement result. The connection between quantum mechanics and consciousness has ever since been a nagging, unwelcome, best-to-pretend-it-doesn't-matter sort of skeleton in the physics closet. But new experiments have pried open the closet door. Quantum theory states that it is the act of observing an object to be at a certain place that actually causes it to be there. This is verified in the laboratory. But we ourselves and the world around us are comprised of atoms that are governed by quantum laws. If consciousness is at the heart of quantum physics (and it is), that puts it at the basis of everything.

Recent best-sellers have denounced the evils of religion and proclaimed that science has shown that there is no God. But the human misuse of religions and the existence of God are very different matters. The problem is: What kind of God are we talking about?

In his little pull-no-punches *Letter to a Christian Nation*, anti-God author Sam Harris goes on a romp through the Bible finding example after example of God decreeing things for his followers to do that only a sociopathic, deranged despot would demand. Such things as stoning your bride to death if she proves not to be a virgin; such things as demanding the slaughter of even women and children if they happen to live in the wrong city at the wrong time... and even innocent cattle to boot.

"Destroy it utterly!" says the God of Deuteronomy. Nowadays he would probably issue the command to nuke the enemy city. If that nut-case is God, add me to the ranks of the atheists. But I say with confidence that there will be no retribution coming my way because that God does not exist. He is merely the product of the dark side of the human imagination (which unfortunately is alive and well in certain parts of the world today).

I am proposing a new concept of God, which is actually very old. It is part of the Perennial Philosophy, which is basically a distillation of core religious beliefs throughout the ages. My contribution is to bring this to the attention of a world sorely in need of an uplifting sense of purpose, and to put it in the context of recent scientific discoveries about the exceptional properties of the universe, and the actual scientific evidence for consciousness creating reality at the quantum level.

Aldous Huxley made the heroic effort of collecting and comparing this mystical stream of fundamental metaphysical truths from many cultures and eras in his book *The Perennial Philosophy*. It concerns the nature of reality, the self, and the meaning and purpose of existence. Huxley's book was greatly praised by one of the founders of modern physics, Erwin Schroedinger.

Key tenets of the Perennial Philosophy are:

- The physical universe of matter is not the sole realty. Other non-physical realities exist, which may contain other life-forms. Interestingly, this is consistent with string theory and M-theory at the forefront of modern physics.

- Our human nature has both a material side subject to physical laws, birth, and death, as well as a non-material immortal spirit or soul.
- All humans possess a capacity to intuitively perceive the true multifaceted nature of ourselves and the greater reality. Unfortunately this is pretty dormant in modern society.

But the greatest truth of all is the saying: Thou art that! Here "thou" refers to our own spiritual nature and "that" is God. And therein lies the answer to the great riddle: If God is responsible for creating the universe (in the Big Bang), why in heaven's name did he do this? The answer, I believe, is to experience physical reality in all the diverse ways possible in such a universe. That is why I think that the "just right" laws of physics are really the "just right" ideas of God made manifest, the "great thought" that Jeans proposed.

An infinite intelligence selects an ensemble of compatible ideas that then become the laws of nature of a given universe. The proper combination results in a universe where life can originate and evolve, and the consciousness of God can then experience its potential. This does indeed give us each a great life's purpose: to create God's experience as the incarnations of him in physical form.

I certainly am not claiming that what I am proposing can be proven. Unresolved riddles remain, such as the origin and nature of evil. Free will and karma surely play a role in that conundrum, but when it comes to God's plans, the devil is in the details.

The Jesuit paleontologist Teilhard de Chardin wrote: "Surely we are not human beings having a spiritual experience, but spiritual beings having a human experience." I would modify this to say: We are God having a human experience. This book will explain why this makes sense, is in no way in conflict with science, and has the potential to transform human consciousness.

INTRODUCTION

Has the time finally come for humanity to transform its behavior and raise its consciousness to a new and better level? Is it possible that we can connect with an intelligence whose thoughts created a Universe tailor-made for life? Given the present state of the world this may sound like the most naïve of fantasies. Nonetheless, the idea resonates with many. Millions are buying books such as the runaway best-seller by Eckhart Tolle, *A New Earth*, and countless others offering a similar message of hope and opportunity for mankind.

15

It would be none too soon. The last violent century saw more than 100 million people slaughtered in wars, genocides, and mere crimes of all sorts, large and small, significant or simply overlooked. The madness continues in the new century. And if mankind's cruelty to each other were not enough, we are now facing the first unmistakable signs of planet-wide environmental disaster on our present course and trajectory. A radical shift in our human consciousness may be the only hope we have.

IS THERE ANY CHANCE IT COULD COME ABOUT?

The possibility of such a transformation has been at the core of religious beliefs, though unfortunately more often than not buried or misinterpreted in self-serving ways. I will not promote any specific religion; indeed, I see most organized religions in their present state as part of the problem, not the solution. Instead I will point to the wisdom teachings drawn from the depths of essentially all religions known as the *Perennial Philosophy*, made famous by the 18th-century mathematical genius Gottfried Leibnitz, and published as a compendium in 1945 by Aldous Huxley.

Just as science derives its truths from experiment and careful observation, the Perennial Philosophy derives its truths from the *transcendent experience* that saints and sages, along with countless ordinary men and women, have reported throughout the ages and across varying religions and cultures. When it happens, this experience is so profound that the true reality revealed in those moments becomes absolutely undeniable, more certain than any other knowledge or prior belief. It is the ultimate "Aha, now I get it!" moment. The same truths emerge over and over again with respect to our true nature as both physical and spiritual beings and our relationship to an underlying intelligence that goes by many names in different cultures, but that is really the same.

A Purpose-Guided Universe

On the cover of *A New Earth* is the bold subtitle: *Awakening to Your Life's Purpose.* And there lies the question: Is there a purpose for your life? And not just a decent but transitory purpose such as a successful career, a happy marriage, or even children of whom you can be proud. Those are laudable, but is there an ultimate purpose transcending all others? Is there a purpose that goes beyond a single mortal lifetime? Is there a purpose for all of us human beings, the widespread realization of which could in fact bring about a transformation of human consciousness?

Let me take this question to the ultimate level. Do we live in a purpose-guided Universe? As an astrophysicist I am well aware of the enormity of space and the vast time scales such as the 14 billion years or so since the Big Bang. Purpose for such an enormous "inanimate physical system" as many of my colleagues would put it, seems to many, indeed probably most, scientists as a blatant absurdity. What could it even mean?

But in physics and astrophysics discoveries are being made that point to a fine-tuning of physical laws and constants of nature that, taken together, are conducive to life and evolution. This has become an important issue in astrophysics, something that cannot be overlooked or brushed under the cosmic carpet. There are really only two ways to explain it. One of them involves a purpose-guided Universe.

Imagine a pyramid made up of stacked basketballs. Picture it a thousand feet on each side and a thousand feet high. That's twice as high as the real great pyramid in Egypt. That's as tall as a hundred-story building. To stack such a pyramid would require about a billion basketballs. It's a big number.

Rounding off to the nearest billion, we live on a five-billion-year-old planet in a 14-billion-year-old universe. Our sun is one star amid a few hundred billion others in the Milky Way Galaxy. Our Milky Way Galaxy is one of a hundred billion or so other galaxies in the visible Universe.

That's a lot of billions.

Given this large-scale picture of things, how could there be any purpose in any man or woman's brief life, amounting to perhaps 80 years or so on average, on one obscure planet? That is a question that matters a great deal to most of us.

As noted physicist Freeman Dyson said in his Templeton Prize lecture:

> *The greatest unsolved mysteries are the mysteries of our existence as conscious beings in a small corner of a vast universe. Why are we here? Does the universe have a purpose? Whence comes our knowledge of good and evil? These mysteries, and a hundred others like them, are beyond the reach of science. They lie on the other side of the border, within the jurisdiction of religion.*

Is there a purpose behind the Universe? There are two diametrically opposed answers coming from the two camps of science and religion ensconced on opposite banks of the stream of life. In my view, neither is satisfactory, which is why I propose a third. But first the two opposing views.

There are those who believe in God. In the United States the percentage of the population falling in this category has hovered around 90 percent for decades. The purpose of life for most believers is clear. It is to live the kind of life that will merit the reward of entrance into an everlasting kingdom of heaven. There, presided over by a heavenly grandfatherly patriarch with the able assistance of an angelic bureaucracy, choir, and legion of saints, the righteous will live in eternal bliss. Given the limited human attention span and the propensity to always want the latest and best, it is hard to see how the eternal heaven business can actually satisfy the clientele for that length of time, that is, forever. One might worry that eternity could possibly become tedious. Still, that's the reward, and it's better than life down here…putting the eternity issue aside.

But you had better be careful, because one life chance is all you get in this view. Given the wide disparity of life circumstances and influences, this one shot at getting it right for all eternity may not seem fair. And indeed, I propose that it is most certainly not. That is one reason why I will suggest a more plausible and humane alternative.

On the other side are the secular humanists, meaning those who dislike and reject the idea of a God, who scoff at such a make-believe purpose as getting into heaven. Unfortunately what they can offer in its place in the way of life purpose is rather limited.

The English poet Francis Thompson wrote: "An atheist is a man who believes himself an accident." That does seriously limit the options available for the purpose-of-life question. Life merely for the sake of living is a risky philosophy that could logically lead to nothing greater than an objective of achieving maximum wealth and pleasure here and now. Some people in this camp do come to this conclusion.

Fortunately, though, most have no less altruism than the believers—perhaps even more because there is no expectation of a reward in the afterlife for doing good here. The problem is that in this view all purpose is ultimately transitory. Recall Weinberg's "The more the universe seems comprehensible, the more it also seems pointless." Unfortunately that would carry over to us individually as well.

The purpose I propose that life has is a grand one, and even, I think, a logical one. We are the means whereby God experiences his own potential, and this is why the Universe has some of the amazing properties conducive to life that it has. Making the analogy of God as a vast bonfire, we are candles whose tiny flame is the same fire. We are sparks of God living in a physical universe of matter and energy in which we are able to experience things, make things happen, live and love and climb up or ski down mountains and enjoy operas or rock concerts, take your pick. The adventures we literally live out were merely possibilities existing pregnantly in the infinite intelligence that is God prior to the creation of the Universe. You might think of the Universe as some of God's thoughts, his daydreams. With the right combination of thoughts providing the basis, the laws of nature, a Universe capable of hosting life becomes possible. God then enriches himself by living through all the life-forms that the Universe can provide…us included. Why shouldn't God get to enjoy the World Series or the Super Bowl or the Indy 500 through the enthusiasm of us fans? Of course, first you have to dream up a universe. God can do that.

In this view heaven is not a place, it is a state of reunion with God from whom our consciousness has temporarily and deliberately separated itself to make physical existence and all its richness possible. The purpose of life is to let God make his own potential real. And of course this cannot be limited to human experience. God in this view seeks the experience of all living things on this planet and wherever else life might exist and whatever else it might be like.

Kaballah scholar Daniel Matt writes in his *God and the Big Bang*:

In the beginning, there was Existence alone—One only, without a second. It, the one, thought to itself: 'Let me be many, let me grow forth.' Thus, out of itself, It entered into every being. All that is has itself alone. Of all things it is the subtle essence. It is the truth. It is the Self. And you are that.

Or from a much more ancient text from India cited by Matt:

He manifested Himself as creation. It is He alone who is born into the world. He lives as all beings; it is only Him everywhere.

NOT INTELLIGENT DESIGN

Let me be clear. This has nothing to do with so-called Intelligent Design. In the view I propose, *Darwinian evolution is essential for fulfilling God's purpose*. The unpredictability and novelty afforded by evolution is absolutely necessary; otherwise existence would be a preordained puppet show. It is the peculiar character of the Universe itself—an issue that has come to the fore in astrophysics—and its origin in the Big Bang that I attribute to an infinite intelligence, not the microengineering of life-forms. It is, in fact, a more impressive feat of intelligence to dream up a few essential laws that can give rise to a universe in which life can evolve, than it would be to tinker around designing creatures like Santa in his workshop.

One might worry about how this view of human beings—and all other life-forms—as extensions of God jibes with our own sense of separation from God. Perhaps even more problematic is the existence of evil. It is evident that there have been—and continue to be—some really rotten characters on this planet: despots, predators, and others who care about no one but themselves. How can they be God in human form? You cannot blithely brush aside things such as the holocaust.

The answer, I believe, lies in our being born into life with free will and with amnesia with respect to our true nature as spiritual beings. In order for the life experience to be potentially rich and original it is necessary to arrive on Earth with a new start. We enter physical life with no memories of the existence we had before birth nor of other lives we may have lived. We acquire an ego that sees ourselves exclusively as the bodies we currently inhabit, separate from others, separate from God. Couple that with our free will to live as we choose, and the possibility of some humans turning to evil becomes ever present. Free will can be a loaded gun.

Some people claim to have at least glimpses of other lives they have lived. Such claims should always be treated with a healthy skepticism—healthy meaning an open-minded willingness to examine the evidence, not mere scoffing. Some are likely to be spurious products of the imagination, but such anecdotal evidence does support the idea that our spiritual and physical history goes beyond one lifetime. The lifework of the late Prof. Ian Stevenson, a University of Virginia psychiatrist and researcher, actually provides forensic evidence supporting the memories of some children who recall a former life. His numerous books and research articles are eye-opening for their thoroughness and rigor, and even moved Carl Sagan to write in his *The Demon Haunted World* that this evidence was worthy of consideration.

That such a view of many lives strikes people in Western society as preposterous is more cultural conditioning than anything else. It would certainly provide a rational basis for understanding how Mozart could play minuets flawlessly at age 4 and write a full-fledged symphony at age 8: Presumably that was not his first life as a musician.

If more than one life is too challenging a concept, set it aside for the time being. But it is fair to ask the question: *Does the idea of getting one shot at life, perhaps in good circumstances, perhaps in bad, and based on that going to an eternal reward or punishment really make more sense? How could such a system be consistent with a just and fair God?*

Back to the question of evil. If we are to believe in a God, we would surely like for him or her to be benevolent and merciful in addition to all-knowing and all-powerful, omniscient and omnipotent. How could he or she tolerate the cruelty that some inflict on others (including on animals) and still merit our respect as a kind and loving God?

What I am proposing—and it is no original idea of mine—is that God chooses to deliberately stay off the playing field in order to let freedom of choice create the new and original experiences that the Universe affords and that God seeks through us. By this I do not mean that God is inaccessible to us; rather that he does not interfere in the evolutionary process and the workings of nature. If we are actually sparks of God, we can cultivate a relationship with him through prayer, or meditation, or just talking to an invisible friend. Working creatively together with God we can to some extent shape our present reality and our future. Clearly we cannot just create any reality we want, but the power of our intention to shape what happens in our lives should not be dismissed. But as for divine meddling in the day-to-day workings of the world—God lets nature and evolution operate independently. The unplanned novelty that leads to is, after all, the objective.

In his book *God After Darwin* Harvard theologian John Haught makes a compelling case for Darwinian evolution being a necessity for the origin of new, autonomous, and unforeseen life-forms. For evolution to work requires God to voluntarily relinquish control, and set aside his omnipotence in the arena of life. I would argue that allowing evil as an undesirable but perhaps inevitable consequence of free will is also an unfortunate necessity.

Perhaps those of us who have chosen life on Earth are the hardy, adventurous souls willing to risk the dangers of coming into an environment where evil exists, and in some cases even predominates and threatens us. Perhaps that is the path of the warrior to spiritual evolution. Certainly I would like to think so.

But that does not give evil a free pass. Whatever we do, in my view, has consequences, and these consequences almost certainly transcend one lifetime.

I don't pretend to know what has become or will become of a monster such as Hitler or an abomination such as Stalin, responsible for millions of deaths and untold suffering, or the deranged suicide-bombing lunatics waging war against civilization today. Likely there will be many lives of atonement and compensation. But whereas my emotion might wish for them to have lowly lives as cockroaches or slugs for every human life whose suffering they caused, I don't think that such regression is possible. My view is that we come back into life at the same level, as a human being, or perhaps progress upward. There may be wondrous, advanced alien civilizations out there that we could deserve to be born into someday if we evolve to an appropriate level. A peaceful, rational place like Mr. Spock's Vulcan appeals to me. I'm not the Klingon type. Pure speculation, of course.

Regardless of precisely how it works, I propose that evil does get its due, not from the direct action of a judgmental God, but from a karmic balance built into the system. I see karma as a kind of spiritual conservation law, cosmic rules of balance and compensation functioning perhaps as autonomously as gravity does here. There are many billions of years remaining for the Universe. I suggest that this affords ample time for even the worst evildoers to compensate, and effectively be punished, for their transgressions. For some of the worst it may deservedly be a most unpleasant fate.

THREE DIFFERENT POSSIBILITIES

But why take any of this seriously at all? Is it not just wishful thinking that there is a purpose to the Universe and a purpose to our lives? What an imagination we humans have! And let's not forget conceit. Sparks of God indeed. Bah, humbug. Where's the evidence?

Some remarkable discoveries have emerged in astrophysics during the past 20 years or so. There are numerous laws and constants of nature, discussed in detail in Chapter 3, whose properties and values could have been radically different, for all we know. Instead, all together, they are tuned in such a way as to make life possible. This fortuitous fine-tuning is not in dispute. It is a recognized "problem" in astrophysics that is in need of an explanation. Not surprisingly, books are written on it by prominent mainstream scientists.

There are three possibilities to explain, or explain away, the fine-tuning:

1. It's just a lucky accident that the laws and constants are what they are. Of course, because we would not be here if they weren't, that part of the mystery is solved. But why the Universe should have the properties it does in the first place is just something we have to accept as given, a fluke.

2. It's a matter of statistics. All sorts of universes exist with different laws and constants. There may even be an infinite number of other universes. All these hypothetical universes together are called a multiverse. But that is just a convenient label. No one knows what kinds of universes a multiverse might contain, and it is all pure theory, no evidence. In the multiverse explanation, we live in a "just right" universe because we could not exist in any other one. In fact, some are so eager to explain away our "just right" conditions that they take our very existence as proof that there must be a multiverse of universes.

3. It's a matter of intelligence. The laws and constants were determined with a purpose in mind: for all sorts of life-forms to evolve, thereby affording the intelligence behind it all the opportunity to experience its creative potential in a tremendous diversity of creatures—us included.

Possibility 1 is not capable of any further elaboration. It could be true but is a dead end in terms of further exploration.

Possibility 2 is quite logical and obviously consistent with science. It's the one you will find in the mainstream popular science books. The problem is that you have to hypothesize a vast, perhaps infinite number of other universes.

These hypothetical universes are ones we will never be able to detect because, being different, their laws of nature are incompatible with ours. That is required to make the statistical argument work. You need a huge, perhaps infinite sample. With a big enough sample the unlikely possibility—a Goldilocks's just right universe, like ours—becomes inevitable. Statistics are wonderful.

Still, the numbers of other universes needed for the statistics to come out right are huge. In his book *The Cosmic Landscape* Stanford physicist and father of string theory Leonard Susskind comes up with the figure of ten to the 500th power (10^{500}) for the number of other universes. That's one followed by 500 zeroes. By comparison to that, the number of atoms in the entire Universe is insignificant (only 1 followed by around 80 zeroes).

It is a pretty big leap of faith to believe in such a multitude of other unseen universes. To me it's a bigger assumption than one intelligence being behind it all. The other issue with this possibility is its causation. One might argue that quantum laws somehow resulted in some vast fluctuation that gave rise to a multiverse of universes. That got us off and running. But if so, some kind of quantum laws had to pre-exist. After all, no laws, no fluctuations. There appears to be no escaping starting with something that just "is"; don't ask why it is or how it came about.

Possibility 3 is as logical as possibility 2. In that case there is an intelligence behind the beginning of our universe. The fact of the matter is that there is no rational way to decide between the two possibilities. But I would argue that the mystical and prayerful experiences of mankind throughout the ages provide not proof, but at least evidence that this may be the better choice. In this view it is a transcendent intelligence that pre-exists, outside space and time.

Who or what made the primordial laws?

Who or what made the intelligence?

No one, because if someone or something did, we have simply not regressed far enough, so dig deeper. The point is, you either accept something, following the logic of Aristotle, as the original uncaused cause...or you are stuck with an infinite regress. That's true whether it is quantum laws or God at the root of things. In terms of causation, quantum laws have no particular edge over an intelligence.

But there is more to consider. Yet another discovery is pointing at least indirectly toward an intelligence underlying the Universe. The history of this discovery goes back to a 1935 attempt by Einstein and two of his coworkers to disprove one of the most significant consequences of quantum mechanics: the Heisenberg uncertainty principle. Einstein believed that quantum theory, including the uncertainty principle, implied what he termed "spooky action at a distance." By this he meant that distant objects can have a direct influence on each other not limited by the speed of light. Einstein thought this was absurd. It violates the laws of special relativity. Einstein could not accept quantum mechanics for that reason.

As it turns out, it took nearly 50 years, long after Einstein's death, for his attempt to disprove quantum mechanics to itself be disproven. Spooky action at a distance is part of quantum theory and points to a fundamental role for consciousness.

The experiment that proved Einstein wrong was a measurement of the so-called Bell inequality, discussed in Chapter 8. The Bell inequality addresses the issue of whether certain quantum properties exist independently prior to measurement, or whether the properties are actually created by the measurement. The first Bell inequality experiment happened in 1982. Physicists Bruce Rosenblum and Fred Kuttner state in their *Quantum Enigma: Physics Encounters Consciousness*:

> *As a result of Bell's theorem and the experiments it stimulated, a once "purely philosophical" question has now been answered in the laboratory. There is a universal interconnectedness. Einstein's "spooky interactions" do, in fact, exist. Any objects that have ever interacted continue to instantaneously influence each other. Events at the edge of the galaxy influence what happens at the edge of your garden. Though these effects are completely undetectable in a normally complex situation, they now get attention in industrial laboratories because they may also make possible fantastically powerful computers.*

Then, in 2007, a yet more profound result emerged from the physics laboratory. A new and even more probing version of the Bell inequality was carried out in the prominent Quantum Optics Laboratory at the University of Vienna and published in *Nature*. This experiment demonstrated that even "spooky action at a distance" was not sufficient to account for the new observations. The property of "local realism" also needed to be sacrificed. Local realism is the assumption that all objects must possess pre-existing values for any possible measurement, prior to the measurement being made. This was shown to be false. Imagine checking a thermometer and finding it to be 72 degrees outside. We naturally assume that it was 72 degrees before we looked, but on the quantum level that would not be true. Making the measurement brings about the reality. In other words, as reported in the weekly science magazine, *New Scientist*,

"...there is no reality independent of measurements.... Rather than passively observing it, we in fact create reality."

Local realism—which now appears to be disproven— maintained that whatever we measure in an object was there to begin with, even though we might not have been aware of it until we made the measurement. Take an analogy. An apple was found to contain 10 apple seeds after we sliced it open. Were they there all along? Local realism said yes. The new quantum experiment says no. The act of slicing open the apple resulted in the 10 seeds appearing there. (This, of course, does not really happen with apples. We are considering golden delicious quantum apples.)

With local realism overruled, does consciousness create reality? These latest discoveries have now moved the question from the realm of philosophy into the quantum physics laboratory. The virtually inescapable conclusion now is that consciousness does create reality. If that is the case, it makes it far less plausible to view consciousness as merely an epiphenomenon of the brain. Consciousness needs to be something greater than a mental illusion created by brain chemistry. Consciousness is the primary stuff.

I propose that the consciousness creating reality in the physics laboratory and the consciousness creating the reality of our lives are a reflection of a transcendent consciousness that gave rise to the Universe itself. Certainly I am not claiming that we have now found God in the physics laboratory. But we do now have telltale signs pointing in that direction.

SCIENCE
AND
RELIGION

Can science and organized religion be reconciled? I would say that the answer is no. Religions are generally rigid institutions each with its own specific set of rules regarding what is right and wrong. Organized religions come with an organizational power and profit structure. Then there is a particular and sometimes idiosyncratic cast of otherworldly characters ranging from only one—God alone—to thousands of lesser gods, angels, demons, saints and other entities, almost always including that one really bad villain to tempt and plague the congregation: the devil. It can be a confusing lot.

Clearly there are serious contradictions among the various religions concerning God and our own nature and destiny. How can you resolve the fact that one religion tells you one thing and a different one says the opposite? Logic, alas, fails.

Now there are a few religions that are virtually dogma- and devil-free, and benign enough that a bona fide, skeptical rocket scientist could attend services, get a bit of Sunday morning inspiration, and even drop a modest check into the collection basket without feeling a twinge of guilt. I would put a church such as, say, Unity, in that category. In fact, the very name indicates why a church like that poses little, if any, conflict with science: It is based on the notion of uniting the best of various beliefs with an open mind rather than claiming sole authority over the truth. Most religions are far more finicky about the requirement to believe specific things...which inevitably wind up contradicting equally strident claims of other religions.

And there are, unfortunately, religions at the far extreme that are grossly at odds even with sane civilized behavior, and cast doubt on the future of the human race. A religion that claims that there is a God who will reward you in heaven for incinerating other human beings down here is not merely deranged and insane, it is a threat to civilization. Reconciliation in such a case is out of the question.

But the reconciliation of science and spirituality is a different matter. That is not only possible, it is essential.

In this book, and in my previous one, *The God Theory*, I propose a concept of God that from my perspective as an astrophysicist in no way contradicts scientific knowledge, and in particular those three pillars: origin of the Universe in a Big Bang some 13.7 billion years ago; a 4.6-billion-year-old

Earth; and Darwinian evolution of life-forms. And there is also no contradiction between what I will call *The God Theory* and the laws of physics, including of course the special and general relativity theories propounded by Einstein.

Moreover, the concept of God I propose does not crash on the rocks of such problems as: How to justify the seemingly undeserved hardships or even horrors that sometimes fall on really good people for no discernable reason?

But is there a need to invoke the concept of God at all?

An Infinite Number of Universes vs. One Great Intelligence

It has been discovered in physics and astrophysics during the past two decades or so that certain properties of the Universe and laws of nature, when looked at together, are remarkably conducive to life arising. This is now well established as something in need of an explanation, and a number of books have been written by prominent scientists such as cosmologist Sir Martin Rees, and Stanford physicist and pioneer of string theory Leonard Susskind, that seek to explain this.

Their argument is that if our Universe has especially life-friendly properties, that has to be a matter of statistics. It has to be chalked up to the odds of chance. In other words, there must be a huge number of other universes whose properties are different from ours, and from each other, and therefore our Universe is not special in any way. It's just that we could never have arisen in any of those less friendly universes, so of course we find ourselves in this one, and thus it looks like a miraculous thing...but it's not at all.

Think of it this way: How likely is it that if you roll six dice at once, they will all turn up sixes? Not very probable. But if you get to toss the six dice a million times, it's bound to happen.

As to how many other universes there must be for this kind of statistical solution to the Goldilocks mystery of the "just right" universe, the estimate ranges from 10 to the 500th power (again, one followed by 500 zeroes) to a literally infinite number. The "lower" estimate results from certain parameters in string theory, and therefore is liable to change (probably to a still higher value). It is, in any case, an unfathomably large number.

That statistical argument is rational, and one can certainly accept it as an explanation of the apparently special properties of our Universe. But is it any more rational than the possibility that our Universe really is special because it is the product of a great intelligence? In my view, both are equally rational. Take your pick. If you truly cannot stomach the idea of a great intelligence, the statistical solution is available to prevent heartburn. But it is neither fair, nor scientifically defensible, to reject the other.

One often hears the objection: well then, where did this intelligence come from? The only possible answer is that it came from nowhere...it pre-exists...it had no beginning... it had no source. If it did, we should skip it and concern ourselves with the ultimate source. Why waste time and philosophical head-scratching over something intermediate? That line of thinking just leads to an infinite regress, a bottomless pit. You do have to start somewhere.

Of course the view that vast numbers of universes arose out of nothing is on no firmer ground. I would argue that that too requires that something pre-exist, namely quantum laws or laws of some sort. If quantum fluctuations are seen as the origin of things, then quantum laws must pre-exist. Where did those come from? It's the same problem.

BELIEF SYSTEMS

In his book *The Universe in a Single Atom: The Convergence of Science and Spirituality*, the Dalai Lama discusses ancient Buddhist concepts about the origin and nature of the Universe. Not surprisingly these consist of rather quaint cosmologies and rudimentary laws of "physics" that are now quite incompatible with what we have discovered in astrophysics. The Dalai Lama makes it very clear that when scientific investigations result in tested and proven modern concepts, those must supersede the old Buddhist notions. Buddhism ascribes authority to experience first, reason second, and scripture last. Direct observation comes out on top. Science trumps tradition and dogma. Would that other religions and religious leaders took such an enlightened position. It would be a saner world.

But it cuts both ways. When scientific investigations point to a finely tuned Universe, scientists should be as open as the Dalai Lama to possible interpretations that challenge the prevailing scientific worldview. It is certainly fair, and even called for by the scientific method, to hypothesize about the possibility of infinite numbers of other universes so as to explain why ours is seemingly special, but is not really. That could be the answer and might someday result in Nobel prizes (and perhaps the equivalent to our 10-dimensional colleagues in the other string-theory universes who have sleuthed out the existence of us in some analogous fashion). But it is intellectually dishonest to discount out of hand the possibility that our Universe appears special because, well, it happens to be special.

The flat-out rejection of that possibility comes from an assumption that reductionism and materialism can be the only sources of true knowledge. Materialism means that the only thing that is real is matter, and that includes energy, because, as Einstein showed, matter can be created from energy and energy from matter...and together they are all there is. Reductionism means that the properties of anything can be explained by looking at the workings of the pieces, an extreme example being that my thoughts can ultimately be explained by analyzing the motions of atoms in my brain.

The Dalai Lama had this to say about reductionist materialism:

Underlying this view is the assumption that, in the final analysis, matter, as it can be described by physics and as it is governed by the laws of physics, is all there is. Accordingly, this view would uphold that psychology can be reduced to biology, biology to chemistry, and chemistry to physics. My concern here is not so much to argue against this reductionist position (although I myself do not share it) but to draw attention to a vitally important point: that these ideas do not constitute scientific knowledge; rather they represent a philosophical, in fact a metaphysical, position. The view that all aspects of reality can be reduced to matter and its various particles is, to my mind, as much a metaphysical position as the view that an organizing intelligence created and controls reality.

THE PROBLEM

Even though it has been many years since Carl Sagan, in collaboration with his talented wife, Ann Druyan, produced the magnificent Cosmos series broadcast on PBS, this is still the pinnacle of a scientifically grandiose vision of the Universe. It is truly an inspiration, but an inspiration of a limited sort. Yes, we are part of something immense and uplifting when viewed from a cosmic perspective. But from a human perspective it is problematic. If we are just chemical machines with an illusion of consciousness destined for oblivion after an average lifespan of perhaps 80 years, where is the inspiration? Are we not dwarfed in both space and time by the enormity of the Universe and its billions of future years? Where is there a purpose for us?

Radical scientific materialism can offer a stupendous vista of the inanimate, but leaves us humans with a narrowness of vision whose end result, when confronted honestly, can hardly be other than nihilism. At least nihilism in the limited sense that existence is ultimately bereft of purpose as far as our own life is concerned.

To again quote the Dalai Lama:

In this view many dimensions of the full reality of what it is to be human—art, ethics, spirituality, goodness, beauty, and above all consciousness—either are reduced to the chemical reactions of firing neurons or are seen as a matter of purely imaginary constructs. The danger then is that human beings may be reduced to nothing more than biological machines, the products of pure chance in the random combinations of genes, with no purpose other than the biological imperative of reproduction.

In his later writings Sagan himself intimated that there might possibly be more to reality than is permitted by the dogma of scientific materialism, and interestingly he refers specifically to the past life research of Ian Stevenson. In his *The Demon Haunted World* Sagan writes:

> *At the time of writing there are three claims in the ESP field which, in my opinion, deserve serious study: (1) that by thought alone humans can (barely) affect random number generators in computers; (2) that people under mild sensory deprivation can receive thoughts or images "projected" at them; and (3) that young children sometimes report the details of a previous life, which upon checking turn out to be accurate and which they could not have known about in any way other than reincarnation. I pick these claims not because I think they're likely to be valid (I don't), but as examples of contentions that might be true.*

STRING THEORY

For about two decades the study of fundamental physics, the investigation of the four forces (electromagnetism, gravity, and the strong and weak nuclear forces and the attempt to unify them) together with the identification of elementary particles and their properties, has been dominated by string theory and its newer extension called M-theory. The idea is that all the elementary particles such as electrons, neutrinos, and quarks are assumed to be different vibration states of an incredibly tiny one-dimensional thing called a string.

String theory is a highly mathematical subject. In fact, it may be fair to say that it is more properly seen as an extremely esoteric branch of mathematics. Its relationship to the real world of physics is the suggestion, based on relationships buried in the mathematics, that gravity might be unified with the other three forces, and that all the apparently different particles that have been discovered in the past century or so are just one kind of string vibrating differently. That is the hope, a hope strong enough to have created a community of string theorists numbering about 1,500 physicists busy as bees writing papers that even other physicists cannot honestly claim to understand in any detail.

A pair of recent books, *Not Even Wrong: The Failure of String Theory and the Search for Unity in Physical Law*, by Columbia University mathematician Peter Woit, and *The Trouble With Physics: The Rise of String Theory, the Fall of Science, and What Comes Next*, by Lee Smolin, a prominent theoretical physicist and string-theory expert at the Perimeter Institute in Canada, argue that physics has lost its way in the mathematical jungle of string theory.

There are at least two major problems. A string would be as small compared to an atom as an atom is to the Solar System. As a consequence, no direct detection of a string has ever been made. Indeed there is no plausible experiment known today that could conceivably detect a string. The "atom smashers" that have detected subatomic particles for decades are useless for detecting a string. The entire power output of all the power plants on Earth would fall billions of time short of having enough strength to create a single string in a particle collider. Let us say that the hope for experimental verification is rather dim.

The second problem is astonishing. The mathematics of string theory requires the existence of several additional dimensions beyond the three dimensions of space and one of time that we are used to living in. The number of additional dimensions ranges from six or seven to as many as 22. In classical string theory these dimensions are "compactified," meaning they are rolled up into tiny loops of dimensional space. In M-theory some dimensions are compactified and some are not; that is, some may be like our own dimensions in extent, but with possibly radically different properties. Think of the difference between space and time; both are dimensions, but their properties are quite distinct. A minute and a meter are rather different.

The point is not to criticize string or M-theory per se. The issue is one of belief. As the dust jacket of Peter Woit's book says:

What happens when scientific theory departs the realm of testable hypothesis and comes to resemble something like aesthetic speculation, or even theology?... string theory is just such an idea.

So we have the situation that certain facts cry out for an explanation. An explanation is found, but it requires assuming the existence of one or more things for which there is no evidence whatsoever in the world of experience. And unfortunately there turns out to be no scientific test possible for the proposed explanation. This is where taking things on faith and seeing where that leads is the only recourse, which is what the vast community of string theorists is doing. But the danger is that the underlying hypothetical foundations of the theory might become articles of faith.

I suggest that the existence of strings and additional dimensions of space as a unifying explanation of the basis of physics on the one hand, and the existence of an intelligence as a unifying explanation of the apparent fine-tuning of our Universe on the other, are not that different philosophically and metaphysically. In fact, there is even a certain degree of tentative mutual support.

In the extension of string theory called M-theory, it is taken for granted that other universes with completely different properties and laws are liable to exist. These universes with their own sets of laws might be separated from ours by tiny distances in another dimension. And if such adjacent universes exist, there is no reason to deny the possibility that the equivalent of life-forms would exist therein, whatever that may mean when "their laws of physics" may be beyond our imagination.

Mystical traditions speak of other non-physical realms with other kinds of beings. M-theory requires the existence of universes with different laws that could in principle host different kinds of beings. There is a curious confluence here, one that is almost humorous given the tendency of materialists to sneer at the supernatural. Perhaps some clever string theorist will yet resolve the vexing perennial question of how many angels can dance on the head of a pin…in various M-theory universes.

HAVING FAITH

In his book *The God Delusion* Richard Dawkins contrasts dogmatic faith in a holy book versus reasoning informed by scientific evidence. He writes:

Fundamentalists know that they are right because they have read the truth in a holy book and they know, in advance, that nothing will budge them from their belief…. The book is true, and if the evidence seems to contradict it, it is the evidence that must be thrown out, not the book. By contrast, what I, as a scientist, believe (for example, evolution) I believe not because of reading a holy book, but because I have studied the evidence.

His point is entirely correct. By contrast with a holy book, a science book can, and does, change as new experiments, observations, or other evidence come to light. Evidence that can be objectively verified trumps revelation, a position that even the Dalai Lama espouses. Indeed, even a fundamentalist might say that scientific evidence trumps revelation...provided it is some other religion's revelation (and therein lies the revelation problem).

Unfortunately things are not as objective and free of preconceptions as Dawkins would have us believe. Our Universe has numerous characteristics that together make for a highly unlikely fine-tuning of properties. This is considered by scientists to be serious and significant enough to warrant an "explanation." Apart from the "it is just a lucky accident explanation" we are left with only two possibilities. Either the properties of our Universe are special because they are indeed the product of an intelligence...or they are just the outcome of statistics. But the latter view requires the existence of a vast, perhaps infinite number of other unseen universes with properties different from our own.

There is simply no scientific way to resolve which explanation is correct: mere statistics or an intelligence with a purpose. Both require the acceptance of something major beyond current science. Recall that many of the other universes in the multiverse statistical argument would have to be radically different from our own to be consistent with the statistics of random properties. That being the case, there might even be intelligent universes in the mix. This would certainly blur the choice between the two explanations. In both cases we would wind up having to accept the existence of realms beyond the conventional physical, that is beyond space and time as we know it. What is the difference between an extradimensional alien being (string theory) and a supernatural or angelic being (religion) other than terminology? Encountering either one would be a shock.

To reject the explanation of an intelligence behind the origin of our Universe simply because one believes that there cannot conceivably be such an intelligence is really no different from faith in the equivalent of a holy book. In this case the faith is in reductionist materialism. Positing the existence of perhaps infinite other universes as a possible explanation is legitimate. But to argue that that *must* be true because the alternative of an intelligence just *cannot* be true is simply to worship at the altar of reductionist materialism. That is how the practice of science can morph into the faith of scientism.

A Better Notion of God

There are conceptions of God that are laughable; there are conceptions that are horrible. Both are at the root of the problem scientists tend to have with the very idea of a God. But it is also possible to have a reasonable conception of God (which I propose is the case for *The God Theory*).

Various surveys have shown that the majority of scientists are atheist, meaning not just doubting whether a God might exist, but actively believing with certainty that there is no God. This is far higher than that of the population at large. A major factor in this disbelief is the kind of entity that comes to mind when one thinks *God*.

A God whose existence or actions directly contradict laws of physics and the known structure of the Universe should be ruled out. Of course there is no way to disprove with 100-percent certainty that some kind of God littered a 6,000-year-old Earth with phony fossils to fool the arrogant archaeologists, but this strikes me as incredibly silly, and if it really were the case we would be in big trouble with this kind of crooked God in charge of things.

A God who exists and maintains a heaven somewhere in the Universe is also a non-starter. If God is a being made of matter, where did the matter come from?

On physical arguments we need a God who is not made of matter, not confined to a Universe, not bound by space and time, because if constrained by these things rather than being the source of these things… he/she/it would not be a real God.

But there are also moral and ethical requirements on the kind of God that scientists—and I myself—can take seriously.

I reject a God who hates, who is vindictive and jealous, who revels in bloodshed or arbitrarily reveals the truth and grants salvation to some select group at the expense of all others. Today, the consequences of the worst possible misconception of God are tragically evident in the fanatics who have perverted the word *martyr* to glorify the murderer, if this were the best we could come up with as a conception of God, I too would be a rabid atheist.

CONSCIOUSNESS CREATING REALITY

One of the things I argue in this book is that quantum mechanics, especially in light of a recent breakthrough experiment measuring the so-called Leggett inequality that supersedes the famous Bell inequality (see Chapter 8), necessarily includes consciousness. It does so to the extent that we can now legitimately claim that consciousness creates the observed reality at the quantum level. This of course has the profoundest of implications for our own macro-reality of everyday life because everything is built upon a quantum basis.

If consciousness is the basis of reality, then it is plausible that a transcendent consciousness is the underlying cause of the Universe. This cannot be proven but it is no less logical a conclusion than the one from mainstream science, which asserts that the Universe, with its surprising life-conducive properties, is merely the result of statistics.

And if that is the case I propose that the motivation of this great intelligence is the seeking of experience in a physical realm. This brings mankind—and all other life-forms here and throughout the Universe—into the picture. I propose to explore our nature as manifestations of this intelligence.

Far from surrendering the rationality and critical thinking that underpins science, it is essential to apply those tools to consideration of the circumstantial evidence for the existence of a transcendent intelligence behind the origin of the Universe. To those who bombastically assert that there is nothing on the side of spirituality worth consideration, let me cite Werner Heisenberg, a man who certainly knew science in depth:

I have never found it possible to dismiss the content of religious thinking as simply part of an outmoded phase in the consciousness of mankind, a part we shall have to give up from now on. Thus in the course of my life I have been repeatedly compelled to ponder on the relationship of these two regions of thought, for I have never been able to doubt the reality of that to which they point. (Scientific and Religious Truth, *1973)*

2

QUANTUM REALITY

A recent query on Amazon.com for books having the word "quantum" in the title yielded nearly 20,000 hits. The term has been usurped from physics and attached to everything from making money (*Quantum Success: The Astounding Science of Wealth and Happiness*) to healing (*Quantum Healing* and too many others to mention) to leadership (*Quantum Leadership: A Textbook of New Leadership*) to golf (*Quantum Golf: The Path to Golf Mastery*). (There is even a *Quantum Zoo*, but this is actually a good book with a whimsical title by respected science writer Marcus Chown. Its subtitle is *A Tourist's Guide to the Never-Ending Universe*.)

Physicists may snicker at such nonsensical linkages with things having nothing to do with quantum physics, but it is books with titles like *Quantum Theology* or *Quantum Faith* or anything purporting to connect quantum physics with Eastern metaphysics or God that make their blood boil and bring out the skeptic sledgehammers.

Quantum physics as we know it today has nothing to say about God directly. However, it has a great deal to say about the nature of reality and consciousness. And because *The God Theory* proposes that all consciousness is a manifestation of a transcendent consciousness, there is a significant indirect connection.

The book by two physics professors at the University of California, Santa Cruz, Bruce Rosenblum and Fred Kuttner, mentioned previously, has "one of those titles": *Quantum Enigma: Physics Encounters Consciousness*, but in fact it is a serious book based on absolutely mainstream quantum physics that tackles the role of consciousness head-on. It is based upon a decade of teaching a course to non-science majors at the university.

"Aha," a physicist might exclaim at this point, "anything taught to non-science majors cannot be a serious course, so we can safely and thankfully ignore this."

Not so.

Quantum mechanics is the most successful theory in science. In one particular calculation it has an accuracy of one part in a trillion. That is to say, the agreement between a theoretical calculation and an experimental measurement (on the magnetic strength of a "spinning" electron) is that precise. That's a breathtaking validation.

The mathematics of quantum mechanics behind such a calculation and others can be quite formidable. It involves such bizarre concepts as abstract infinite dimensional spaces containing not things but rather vectors and operators. But in fact none of this mathematical rigmarole matters one bit with respect to the quantum enigma. It is possible for someone with no training whatsoever in mathematics to fully understand the fundamental issue. And conversely it is possible that, as an example, a quantum electrodynamics genius capable of reproducing the mathematics behind the previously mentioned calculation may be naïve enough concerning the fundamentals to think the enigma is solved. The mystery lies not in the numbers, which work out extremely well. The mystery lies in the interpretation behind it, and this can be grasped without mathematics even by an undergraduate, as Rosenblum and Kuttner show.

Here is the enigma, conventionally called the "measurement problem." On the ordinary scale of things our reality seems quite fixed and independent of any attention we pay to it. When a tree falls in a forest, no rational person doubts that the crashing sound occurs whether or not there is anyone to hear it. But in the quantum realm the only logical interpretation of experiments is that the reality is created by the measurement.

The reality that is thought to exist all along whether or not a measurement is made, did not actually exist prior to the measurement.

In their book, Rosenblum and Kuttner discuss in detail the various interpretations proposed in quantum mechanics to get around this. Ultimately they are all unsatisfactory, leaving the conclusion intact that reality is created at the quantum level. As Pascual Jordan, one of the originators of quantum theory said: "Observations not only disturb what is to be measured, they produce it." Referring to a quantum measurement of an atom in a box Rosenblum and Kuttner bluntly state: "The atom wasn't in that box before you observed it to be there."

Experience tells us that one object cannot be in two places at the same time.

Relativity theory tells us that what happens at point A cannot *instantaneously* affect what happens at point B some distance away because nothing can move faster than the speed of light.

Common sense tells us that a real world exists whether or not we consciously pay attention to it.

Quantum mechanics disputes all these intuitions.

But in fact, everything is built upon the quantum level. The structure of the everyday world ultimately is built upon the "unreal until measured" quantum bricks. As Rosenblum and Kuttner write:

"But if quantum theory denies the straightforward physical reality of atoms, it would also seem to deny the straightforward physical reality of chairs, which are made of atoms."

And that is why the two physicists have been warned by colleagues that they are handing their students a loaded gun, philosophically speaking. After all, such thinking might lead the poor students to fall for all sorts of mumbo-jumbo nonsense... of which there is a great deal available. The quantum enigma may lead the students to conclude that consciousness somehow creates physical reality. The quantum enigma is the skeleton that should be left in the closet.

AN IDEAL QUANTUM EXPERIMENT

Let's examine a quantum experiment devised by three preeminent geniuses of theoretical physics: Dr. Moe, Dr. Larry, and Prof. Curly.

Prof. Curly has devised machines that slice or chop pennies in half. A "slice" is a cut lengthwise through a penny, so that we wind up with two thin coins. One has the profile of Abraham Lincoln on one side and nothing on the back. The other coin has the Lincoln memorial on one side and nothing on the back. This is shown in Figure 1.

Sliced   Chopped

Figure 1

A "chop" divides the coin in half very differently, resulting in two "half-moon" pennies. One coin has Lincoln's head; the other has Lincoln's shoulders.

Prof. Curly, being the genius that he is, has two versions of the slicing and chopping machine. One is a classical model and one a quantum model.

In experiment one, Prof. Curly uses the classical machine to slice the penny. The machine, being quite sophisticated, puts one sliced coin in one envelope addressed to Dr. Moe, one in another addressed to Dr. Larry, and labels both envelopes "Sliced." Prof. Curly takes the envelopes out of the machine and puts them out for the mailman to pick up. He then goes to take a nap.

The next day Dr. Moe, who lives in Stoogeburg, and Dr. Larry, who lives 100 miles away in Stoogeville, both get envelopes in the mail. Dr. Moe expects to find a sliced penny inside because that is how the envelope is labeled. He opens his and sure enough, there is a sliced coin inside and it has the Lincoln profile on it. He calls his colleague Dr. Larry, who was still asleep, and sure enough, when he gets his envelope out of the mailbox it contains the backside of the original coin: the Lincoln Memorial.

Dr. Moe calls Prof. Curly and yells at him: "Listen, puddin' head, what kind of silly experiment was that? I got half a coin and Larry got the other half. What does that prove? To which Prof. Curly responds: "Nyuk, nyuk, nyuk...you ain't seen nothin' yet."

In experiment two, Prof. Curly sets the classical machine to "chop." Once again the machine goes to work, turns out two "half-moon" shaped coins, puts one in each of two envelopes labeled "Chopped" and addressed to Dr. Moe and Dr. Larry.

The next day Dr. Moe finds an envelope labeled "Chopped" in his mailbox. Expecting to find a chopped penny inside, sure enough he discovers one with Lincoln's head. He calls his colleague Dr. Larry, who is busy fixing flapjacks for breakfast. Dr. Larry checks his mailbox, finds an envelope labeled "Chopped" and inside there is the other half of the coin with Lincoln's shoulders.

Dr. Moe calls Prof. Curly and yells: "Oh, a wise guy, eh? What kind of silly experiment was that. I oughta punch..." Prof. Curly stops him: "Wait till you see this next one."

It's time for experiment three. This time Prof. Curly fires up the quantum machine. He inserts a coin in the machine. It hums and whirrs and then spits out two sealed envelopes. This time, though, the envelopes are not labeled "Sliced" or "Chopped." Instead they are labeled "Quantum." The mailman picks them up.

The next day Dr. Moe finds an envelope labeled "Quantum" in his mailbox. Just then Prof. Curly calls up:

Curly: *Hey, Moe. Did you get the quantum envelope I sent you?*

Moe: *Yeah, and I'm about to open it.*

Curly: *Don't do that yet. First you've got to decide whether the envelope contains a sliced or a chopped coin.*

Moe: *Are you nuts? Your machine already sliced or chopped it. I can't change that now.*

Curly: *Yes, you can. In fact you've got to decide which one it is to complete the experiment.*

Moe: *Look here, puddin' head. Are you claiming that if I decide the envelope contains a sliced coin, I'll find that inside, and if I decide it's a chopped coin I'll find that inside?*

Curly: *That's right.*

Moe: *Listen here. That's crazy. That would mean that whatever is inside is not quite real.*

Curly: *Nyuk, nyuk, nyuk.*

Moe: *Alright. I say I'm going to find a chopped coin in there. Now can I also decide which half of the coin I'll find? Lincoln's head or Lincoln's shoulder?*

Curly: *No. That's the part you have to discover. Looking to see which one it is, is called the measurement. You get to decide which kind of coin you're going to observe, sliced or chopped, but once you've decided that then chance determines which half it is.*

Dr. Moe decides he will find a chopped coin. He then opens the envelope, and just as he decided, there is a half moon-shaped chopped coin. It turns out to be the Lincoln head half. But now he is confused.

Moe: *Okay, wise guy, it was a chopped coin. But what about the envelope you sent to Dr. Larry? What if he decides his other half is a sliced coin. That would not be the other half of this one?*

Curly: *It's too late for him to do that. Once you've decided which kind of coin you've got, that fixes the outcome in his envelope. He's going to get the correct other half and he can't change that if you decided first.*

Dr. Moe calls Dr. Larry, who was just watching a rerun of *The Three Stooges* on TV. When Dr. Larry opens his envelope, sure enough, it is a chopped coin of Lincoln's shoulders.

Moe: *Fiddlesticks. You just got lucky. Let's do this again a few more times.*

Curly: *Soitanly, nyuk, nyuk, nyuk.*

Needless to say, each time the experiment is done, Dr. Moe finds just the right kind of coin, sliced or chopped, always corresponding to his decision before opening his envelope. And Dr. Larry, who always opens his envelope second, always has the matching half.

WAVES AND PARTICLE

Imagine camping next to a crystal-clear lake in midsummer, high up in the mountains. It is 5 a.m., the Sun has just risen, and your companions are just starting to stir, but you are the first one out of your tent. Everything is calm. There is not even the slightest breeze. The surface of the lake is smooth as glass.

Just for fun you pitch a rock into the still water. Waves radiate out from the impact point of the rock. They keep moving out in several perfect concentric rings until they just fade away.

Now you pitch two rocks with the same hand. They hit the water at exactly the same moment, side by side, three feet apart. Again waves radiate out from each impact point, and when the two rings begin to overlap a pattern is formed that is more complicated than the concentric circles that one rock formed all alone.

In a laboratory you can create similar patterns with light, using a laser pointer and a screen, because light is a wave. If you shine the laser beam through a single slit in a screen (like a single rock hitting the water) you see one kind of pattern on the wall behind the screen. If you shine the laser beam through two slits simultaneously (like two rocks hitting the water side by side) you will get a different pattern on the wall. It is called an interference pattern because the waves coming from each slit interfere with each other. It's the same process as the overlapping of waves in the water.

Actually, the previous passage is only half true. Light does behave just like a wave under some conditions. But under other conditions it behaves like a particle, called a photon. Photons move in straight lines (except in curved space) and do not spread out. The human eye can almost see an individual photon.

If you could turn the laser power level down, down, down, pretty soon it would be emitting light in discrete photons: individual lumps of light. Imagine water streaming from a faucet. When it's running high enough you have a continuous stream of water. Think of this as the analogy of the wave. If you turn down the faucet far enough you will start to get individual drops dribbling out. Think of this as the analogy of the photon. So is water a continuous stream or is it composed of drops? The answer is both. It depends on the circumstances you create.

Now here is the odd thing about light. If you turn the laser down low enough that individual photons emerge, one at a time, and if you keep the laser pointing at two slits in the screen, you can still get a wave-like interference pattern on the wall even if only one photon at a time goes through a slit. You would think that it would take two photons, one going through each slit at the same time to give you an interference pattern...but it doesn't. What is the single photon interfering with if there is no second photon coming through the other slit? Physically there seems to be no mechanism for creating interference, yet if you have two slits and let one photon at a time go through whichever slit it chooses, an interference pattern will still build up one photon at a time. A single photon acts just like it's going through both slits. Common sense seems to fail at the quantum level. Clearly, reality in the quantum world is very strange. The "normal rules" don't seem to apply. This is a clue that ordinary reductionist materialism may not apply.

So let's ask another paradoxical question: if a wave-like thing like light can also act like a particle, can a particle behave like a wave? This was the question a physics doctoral student asked himself in 1922. His name was Louis de Broglie and the answer proved to be yes.

If you want to launch a rocket into space, you calculate how much force, or thrust, your engines will generate on liftoff and if that force is greater than the weight of the rocket...blast-off occurs. The rocket is composed of particles—atoms—and by de Broglie's theory the atoms all have the ability to act like waves, so even the rocket should have wave-like properties. Indeed it does, but the particle-like

properties are so much greater than the wave-like properties that for all practical purposes there is no wave-like behavior. You don't need to worry about the wave-like properties, and that means you can do your rocket engineering
without taking into account quantum physics.

THE WAVEFUNCTION

A quantum-size particle definitely does show wave-like
properties. The calculations that predict what a particle will
do under various circumstances is done according to quantum laws. That involves calculating the "wavefunction" of
a particle. The wavefunction is usually a complex pattern
comprised of overlapping waves. Go back to the rock being
tossed into the lake. Simple concentric rings are emanating
from the point of impact. Follow the ring of waves heading
back towards you on the shore. Once those waves hit obstacles, such as logs and rocks in the water by the shore, the
pattern becomes more and more complicated.

The wavefunction of a particle, such as a single atom, is
similarly an evolving pattern that depends on both the type
of particle and its environment. Because the wavefunction
is a spread-out pattern, it is possible to "catch" some of it in
a quantum box about the size of an atom. In fact, it is possible to catch some of it in one quantum box and some in
another adjacent box.

The million-dollar question is: What is the mysterious
wavefunction? A wavefunction is nothing you can see. It's
not even a "real" field. It is calculated from quantum laws
to predict the outcome of an experiment. Think of it as a
cloud of probability that tells you how likely it is to find a
certain particle at a certain place if you make a measurement. It is tempting to think of the wavefunction as some
kind of a field that surrounds a particle, but that is not the

case. The wavefunction is all there is of the particle. The fact of the matter is, until a measurement is made, there is no particle. When you make the measurement, voila, the wavefunction disappears (collapses) and the particle suddenly appears somewhere in the region that the wavefunction said it should.

Rosenblum and Kuttner make this point over and over: The wave function is identical with the particle.

In quantum theory there is no atom in addition to the wavefunction of the atom. This is so critical that we say it again in other words. The atom's wavefunction and the atom are the same thing; 'the wavefunction of the atom' is a synonym for 'the atom.'

Consider a burning log that is giving off lots of smoke. In fact, so much smoke that the log itself is hidden. All we can see is a cloud of smoke. Think of the smoke as the wavefunction of the log. Thinking like classical physicists we would know that somewhere inside this cloud of smoke there is a burning log. But if we look at this from a quantum perspective, the smoke is all there is because that is all that we see. There is no burning log inside the smoke until we make a measurement, say, by using a fan to blow the smoke aside.

Classically, blowing the smoke aside reveals what was there all along: a burning log. Quantum mechanically blowing the smoke aside *creates* the burning log. This is an extremely important point to grasp: the wavefunction *is* the atom.

If the wavefunction of an atom is spread over two boxes, does that imply the seemingly nonsensical interpretation that a single atom is in both boxes at the same time? The answer is yes. Experiments confirm this. A *Physics News* item from the American Institute of Physics in 2003 carried the headline "3600 Atoms in Two Places at Once." In fact, an atom can even move in two opposite directions at once because that is what a wavefunction can do and, to repeat again, the wavefunction *is* the atom.

But that does not mean that you can actually see a ghostly half an atom inside one of the boxes. The reason is that seeing the atom in one box or the other constitutes making a measurement. Once that measurement is made, that affects the wavefunction (called collapse of the wavefunction) in just such a way as to yield one whole atom in one box or the other. The laws of quantum mechanics are such that you cannot directly experience the ghostly wavefunction even though that literally *is* the atom at the time. Looking inside one of the boxes creates the reality of the atom being there. The wavefunction suddenly transforms into a complete atom.

*Accordingly, before a look collapses a widely spread-out wavefunction to the particular place where the atom is found, the atom did not exist there prior to the look. The look brought about the atom's existence at that particular place—for everyone. (*The Quantum Enigma*)*

Not only does the process of looking—making the measurement—create the present reality, it also creates whatever back history is logically necessary to bridge the time between a previous measurement and the present one. This can be illustrated by the famous Schroedinger's Cat thought experiment...with apologies to cat lovers everywhere.

SCHROEDINGER'S CAT

Imagine a box containing a Geiger counter, a tiny bit of radioactive material, a small flask of hydrocyanic acid linked to a spring-driven hammer...and one inactive, sleepy cat. Assume that there is such a tiny amount of radioactive material that in the course of a minute there is a 50/50 chance that one of the atoms decays. This in turn would cause a signal in the Geiger counter, which trips the hammer, which shatters the flask of hydrocyanic acid, which, alas, kills the cat. (It is rumored that this experiment was suggested by Schroedinger's dog.)

Flourine-17 is a radioactive element. It spontaneously changes (decays) into oxygen-17, and on average this takes about a minute. Now there is no guarantee that a minute is long enough. It could take much longer...on the other hand it could happen after only a few seconds. Let's say that the radioactive triggering device in the cat box experiment contains a single atom of fluorine-17. Assume you get this by extracting a single fluorine-17 atom from a batch and putting it next to the Geiger counter. You then close up the box with the cat soundly asleep.

According to quantum mechanics, as time progresses the wavefunction of the fluorine-17 atom begins to change into partially fluorine-17, partially oxygen-17, the decay product. The change is such that after a minute the wavefunction is half fluorine-17, half oxygen-17. The atom is in a half-and-half state. The more time passes, the more the wavefunction takes on the properties of oxygen-17 and less of fluorine-17. In our experiment, if the wavefunction collapses, the transition is complete and we have an atom of oxygen-17, which triggers the Geiger counter, which trips the hammer, which cracks open the flask, which—unfortunately—kills the cat.

Remember that the wavefunction is really the atom itself that is changing, albeit in an unobservable way. Quantum mechanics forbids seeing any such intermediate state. Once we do decide to observe, that is make a measurement, the observation immediately forces an atomic decision. We will wind up with either an oxygen-17 or fluorine-17 atom. If it is fluorine-17, the act of observation effectively resets the timer governing the decay of fluorine-17.

So at the end of a minute we open the box and find either a sleepy cat or a dead cat. That process of opening the box constitutes making the quantum measurement. The question is, during that previous minute, was the cat alive or dead. Was the cat in a half-and-half state because the wavefunction of the atom was in a half-and-half state?

The quantum answer is...both alive and dead. Until the measurement is made, the wavefunction for the entire system, including the cat, is in an undetermined state, technically called a superposition of states. In one state the atom does not decay, the Geiger counter does not trip the hammer, the flask is unbroken and the cat is snoozing. In the other state the atom has decayed, the Geiger counter has tripped the hammer, the flask has shattered and the cat is out of luck, only eight lives to go. Both situations are equally semi-real.

This is clearly an unreal experiment; the objects are far too big and the time far too long. Cats of the world, you need not worry! Nevertheless the laws of quantum mechanics tell us unambiguously that in principle both contradictory potential realities co-exist during that minute of time. The resolution, the creation of the actual reality, occurs at the moment of measurement. But that moment of measurement also takes one of the two previous potential realities and makes it real. The actual history of that minute is backfilled by the measurement. The cat might have died after only 10 seconds in the box, or just at the moment that we opened the box. There is no way of knowing, but whatever happened during that minute was not determined until the minute we made the measurement.

This creation of reality by measurement including appropriate back history is the skeleton in the closet of quantum physics for those who prefer to view consciousness as just another physical process happening in the brain.

WHEELER'S DELAYED CHOICE EXPERIMENT: IF YOU COME TO A FORK IN THE ROAD—TAKE IT!

The backward-in-time causation in the Schroedinger's cat experiment is certainly intriguing, but it remains a mental experiment. Thankfully for cats everywhere such an experiment cannot actually be carried out, just as we cannot slice or chop coins Stooge-style via quantum observation. In both cases, the mind-challenging implications of these idealized situations are totally real, but the experiments were merely illustrative. Equivalent quantum experiments, of course, have validated the concepts. Amazingly, a recent experiment by a French team, reported in *Science* magazine in 2007, has actually succeeded in making a real measurement of backwards-in-time causation.

The theory behind this delayed-choice experiment was proposed in 1978 by John Archibald Wheeler, an eminent American physicist and collaborator with Einstein.

This is simplistically illustrated in Figure 2. In all cases a photon flies through a pipe from left to right. In (a) the photon encounters a "chooser" that can be set to position 1 or 2. If it is set to 1, the chooser tells the photon that off to the right an interference-type measurement will be made (not shown for simplicity), which means the photon had better get into the proper configuration to allow that to happen. Obediently, the photon splits into two ghostly halves at the fork and each half goes down one of the tunnels. This will create the desired interference pattern.

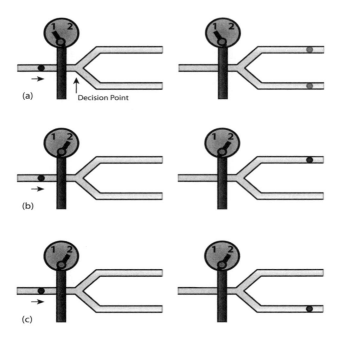

Figure 2

If the chooser is set to position 2, that tells the photon that a detector will measure the emergence of a complete photon out of one or the other of the tunnels. Obediently the photon forks without splitting this time, into one of the tunnels as shown in (b) and (c).

This may seem like pretty weird behavior but cause and effect seem to be okay. But now consider the situations in Figure 3 where (a), (b) and (c) are similar to Figure 2 except for the fact that the chooser does not tell the photon which position it is set to until *after* the photon has moved past the fork. In (a) of Figure 3 the photon splits in two even though it is not told until after the fork point that that is what it is supposed to do. Similarly for (b) and (c) the photon does the appropriate thing for a position 2 setting on the choice of measurement coming up even though it has no way of knowing that setting until after reaching the fork.

The team actually used a random number generator to make the decision on which type of measurement to make. Using a 150-meter path and the ability to do switching in 40

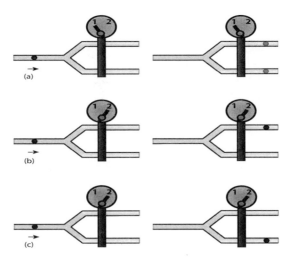

Figure 3

billionths of a second, the team was able to use the random number generator to force the photon to have made its decision prior to knowing what it was going to have to do.

You could argue that the chooser somehow is able to reach back in time to tell the poor photon what is going to happen. Or you might argue that consciousness has the power to act upon the whole system to get what it chooses to measure, damn the details of how. (And by the way, were we to decide to look in on the ghostly half-and-half split photons, what we would see is a single complete photon in one tunnel or the other because seeing is that kind of measurement.)

CONSCIOUSNESS

In Chapter 8, we will see that a new and more sophisticated version of the so-called Bell inequality called the Leggett inequality carried out in the Institute for Quantum Optics and Quantum Information at the University of Vienna and published in *Nature* in April 2007 presents a stunning confirmation of the skeleton in the closet. Reporting on this *New Scientist* said:

Recent experiments led by a group at the University of Vienna, Austria, provide the most compelling evidence yet that there is no objective reality beyond what we observe. This idea, that our measurements create reality, is controversial and scarcely new, but the mounting evidence for it could have major implications in the search for a theory of everything.

To cut to the chase, quantum mechanics is telling us that consciousness creates reality. Naturally this has profound consequences for the interpretation of our own nature, the seemingly fixed reality we take to be our universe, and, yes, even why it may make more sense to trace everything back to a conscious intelligence rather than simply inanimate fields and forces. Next we consider the evidence that key characteristics of our Universe show the signature of conscious purpose.

3

The Finely Tuned Universe

Nothing will come of nothing.
—William Shakespeare, *King Lear*

Is there an intelligence behind the origin of the Universe? Is there a purpose for its existence, and for our individual lives? Or is the Universe simply an accident, something that emerged out of nothing? Perhaps simply one of an infinite number of universes that somehow arose from preexisting quantum laws?

Beginning with the proposition by Nicolaus Copernicus, published in 1543, that the Earth is not the center of the Universe, the idea has taken hold in science that it is most logical to assume that there is nothing special about the Earth or our place in the Universe. This philosophical position is called the Copernican Principle. In spite of the formality of its name it is an assumption, not an established law of nature.

The Copernican Principle is generally true. The Solar System resides in a galaxy comprised of at least 100 billion other stars, the Milky Way Galaxy. The Sun is a fairly average type of star and we are located somewhat near the outskirts of the Galaxy, about 30 thousand light-years from the center. Because the center of the Galaxy shows evidence of a supermassive, star-swallowing black hole, our location is not a bad one. But it is an ordinary one.

We have arrived at a very interesting point in history. It has been discovered during the past 20 years that while our place in the Universe appears to be quite unexceptional, the Universe itself is rather special. This is an insight whose implications are only beginning to be grasped by science, and even less appreciated yet for its implications by the metaphysical or spiritual thinkers of the world. Not surprisingly there are two radically different explanations of this specialness.

A UNIVERSE MADE FOR LIFE

The view I present herein I have called *The God Theory*. This is nothing like Intelligent Design, which proposes that an intelligence created and microengineered life-forms as an alternative to Darwinian evolution. *The God Theory*, on the other hand, as mentioned previously, accepts the reality of the Big Bang some 13.7 billion years ago, a 4.6-billion-year-old Earth, and, importantly, Darwinian evolution as the means for life to develop. It addresses a very deep question that science cannot resolve: Is the Universe itself accidental or purposeful? On this issue the National Academy of Sciences has taken the following official position:

Religions and science answer different questions about the world. Whether there is a purpose to the universe or a purpose for human existence are not questions for science.... Science is a way of knowing about the natural world. It is limited to explaining the natural world through natural causes. Science can say nothing about the supernatural. Whether God exists or not is a question about which science is neutral.

The Universe is an amazingly friendly place for life. This may seem like an odd thing to say, given how dark, empty, and forbidding space is. There is no sunny blue sky, no gentle summer breeze. What did the Apollo astronauts see and experience on their way to and from the moon?

The Sun was shining, but as a harsh, blazing Sun in an absolutely black sky. A Sun that heated one side of the spacecraft past the boiling point of water, while the shaded side of the craft froze at temperatures of more than 100 degrees below zero. And the fact that the spacecraft could travel at speeds of more than 20,000 mph with no resistance was due to the lack of air. Space is a pretty deep vacuum, good for whizzing through but not hospitable to life.

Beyond the solar system conditions are harsher still. Imagine traveling not a mere 180 thousand miles to the Moon, nor even several billion miles to the outermost planets: Uranus, Neptune, Pluto, no longer a full-fledged planet, now just a dwarf planet, but a good outpost at the outer limits of the solar system. Travel instead 10 trillion miles, halfway to the nearest star, Alpha Centauri. Look out your starship window and there you will see the Sun as just another point-like star in a pitch black sky. There is no heat to speak of, no light other than from the pinpoints of stars, and an even more perfect vacuum than that between the Earth and the Moon.

The temperature a thermometer would register is a mere 5 degrees Fahrenheit above absolute zero. That temperature, minus 455 degrees Fahrenheit, comes from the faint glow left over from the Big Bang that started the Universe, a glow that is invisible to the naked eye, but measurable with radio telescopes.

Cold, dark, empty...with trillions of miles of emptiness between stars. How is the Universe friendly to life? The friendliness lies in the laws of nature. There are at least 10 fundamental properties of the Universe that together have just the right values to make life possible.

THE FORCE OF GRAVITY TO THE ELECTRIC (COULOMB) FORCE

The first fortuitous property involves two forces of nature that we experience every day: gravity and electricity. Electricity is produced when electrons stream through a conductor. In every house, electric currents made up of electrons flow back and forth at 60 cycles per second (50 in Europe) through wires and outlets. Electricity works because electrons have a negative charge. Electrons repel other electrons because of this charge. On the other hand electrons attract protons, which are positively charged, with exactly the same strength.

Electrons and protons are particles of matter. That means that in addition to the electric force (called the Coulomb force) there is an almost infinitesimally small force of gravity between electrons and other electrons, or between electrons and protons. It is the ratio of the gravitational force to the electric force that is the first key value setting the stage for life.

If the gravitational force were 10 times stronger than it is, relative to the electric force, stars would be smaller and have shorter lifetimes. Our Sun is about 4.6 billion years old, about halfway through its life. In a universe with a stronger gravitational force—relative to the electric force—the Sun would have burned itself out by now, cutting short the time for evolution of life on the surface of any planets in such a solar system.

And the planets too would be affected. They would likely be smaller and denser, with higher surface gravities. Any creatures that did manage to evolve in spite of the limited time would be far smaller than we are.

Galaxies would also be affected. Our Sun is part of the pinwheel-shaped Milky Way Galaxy containing at least 100 billion stars. But in a Universe with a stronger gravitational force, galaxies would be smaller; stars would be closer together. This has the consequence that stars would sometimes pass closely enough to each other to perturb the orbits of planets. That would likely change the climate of a planet, not a good thing when you want long-term stable conditions for life to evolve.

Between the abbreviated lifetimes of stars, the altered conditions on the surfaces of Earth-like planets, and perturbations by neighboring stars it is unlikely that life as we know it could have arisen if gravity were much stronger than it is relative to the electric force.

And on the other hand, if gravity were much weaker, far fewer stars would form, hence far fewer planets on which life can arise.

THE NUCLEAR FORCE

Stars that serve as suns for hospitable planets are the necessary environments for life. Nuclear reactions power stars. As Einstein discovered in 1905, matter can be converted into energy…and vice versa. This is crucial to the existence of stars. It's where their energy comes from.

Stars begin their lives as huge, contracting clouds of gas, primarily composed of hydrogen. Hydrogen is the simplest element, number one in the Periodic Table. It consists of one proton (the nucleus) and one electron. As the gas compresses due to its own gravity, the gas cloud shrinks to form a round star. It heats up and becomes extremely dense at its core.

Inside the star, electrons are stripped from the protons and move around freely. When the gas achieves a hundred times the density of water and a temperature of 20 million degrees Fahrenheit, nuclear reactions begin. In a multistage process, several hydrogen nuclei (which are just single protons) are converted into helium, the next simplest element whose nuclei consist of two protons and two neutrons. (This is possible because part of the process converts two of the protons into two neutrons.) Figure 4 shows schematically the input and output products of the most prevalent branch of the proton-proton fusion chain powering the Sun.

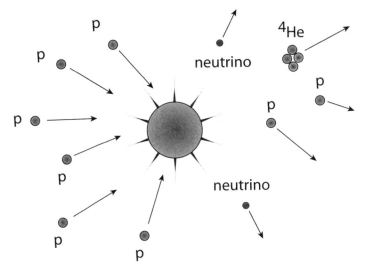

Figure 4

The two protons and two neutrons that make up a helium nucleus are tightly bound by the nuclear force that holds them together. This is different from the hydrogen nucleus, which is just a single proton and thus requires no binding together of protons and neutrons by the nuclear force. It is this binding caused by the nuclear force that releases energy. Another way to look at it is to say that the mass of the resulting helium is slightly less than the sum of the initial hydrogen nuclei, by 0.7 percent. That 0.7 percent loss of mass becomes—via Einstein's $E=mc^2$—the energy that powers a star and causes it to shine.

The hydrogen-to-helium conversion takes place in several steps involving the creation of intermediate products. First there is deuterium, which is heavy hydrogen consisting of a proton and a neutron. Then helium-three, light helium, is created, consisting of two protons and a single neutron.

The strength of the nuclear force is critical for these intermediate products to be created.

Specifically it is the first reaction in the series that is crucial, the one that makes deuterium. Two protons collide and stick together thanks to the nuclear force. Then one of the protons becomes a neutron, and thus you have deuterium. If the nuclear force were 10 to 20 percent stronger than it is, this reaction would have occurred so efficiently in the Big Bang itself that all the hydrogen in the early universe would be converted into deuterium, leaving no hydrogen to power stars, hence no stars.

On the other hand, if the nuclear force were 10 to 20 percent weaker, deuterium would be unstable and the rest of the hydrogen-into-helium process would be short circuited. Stars would never be able to tap in to the nuclear energy that powers them. In that case, stars would likely collapse into black holes instead of shining through liberation of nuclear energy.

THE DENSITY OF MATTER

For thousands of years, the Earth was thought to be at the center of the cosmos. The Sun, the Moon, and five lights in the night sky called planets circled around the Earth at different rates. Constellations comprised of about 10,000 lights called stars moved together around the Earth. This was the Universe of ancient Egypt, Babylon, Greece, Rome, Europe in the Middle Ages. No one knew how big it was, but probably not much more than familiar distances on Earth. And above the firmament of the stars was heaven… with hell presumably deep down in the bowels of the Earth.

The Universe of today is a vastly different place. Even the Solar System is a whole lot bigger than the imagined Universe of antiquity. The outermost reaches of our solar system are several billion miles from the Sun. Then, it is another 25 trillion miles to Alpha Centauri, our nearest stellar neighbor in the Milky Way Galaxy. Our Galaxy has a diameter of about a million trillion miles. There are roughly as many galaxies in the Universe as there are stars in the Milky Way: several hundred billion. And the size of the entire Universe is impossible to grasp except in the abstract terms of numbers: about 100 billion trillion miles.

Born in an unimaginable fireball of trillions of degrees—the Big Bang—the Universe has been expanding for 13.7 billion years. Astronomer Edwin Hubble discovered in the 1920s that the farther away a galaxy is from us, the faster it is receding. Imagine it like a balloon blowing up. Eventually, far enough away, that recession velocity equals the speed of light itself. And that is our wall of visibility: the Hubble horizon. Like a fish trying to swim upstream against a rapid current, the light will never make progress toward us. It will forever recede away. That's as far as we will ever see with our most powerful instruments.

In one sense we know immeasurably more about the Universe than the ancients did. But we also know curiously less. The ancients may not have understood the workings of the Universe, but they surely thought they could see all of it: the Sun, the Moon, five planets, and several thousand stars.

But today, 25 percent of our modern Universe is comprised of dark matter. We can't see it with our best instruments, but there is unmistakable evidence in the gravitational behavior of galaxies and clusters of galaxies that it exists. Something major is influencing the motions of stars and galaxies. We have no idea what it is. It could be new types of particles. It could be something else. No one knows.

Apart from its intrinsic mystery, dark matter is important because it is the major component in determining the average density of the Universe. If you take the stars, the planets, the gas and dust clouds in interstellar space and imagine distributing all their atoms uniformly throughout the Universe, you would wind up with about one single atom on average in a volume the size of a small closet. That's how much is due to the known type of matter.

There is about five times as much dark matter. Both ordinary matter and dark matter exert gravity, which causes an attractive tug on the expanding universe. Knowing how rapidly the Universe is expanding it is possible to calculate just how much matter, ordinary and dark, there would have to be to cause the Universe to stop expanding. That amount of matter is called the critical density, the amount that is just enough to halt the expansion but not quite enough to cause a recollapse of the Universe. If the Universe had on average the critical density, it would expand ever more slowly, stopping altogether at a time infinitely far in the future. More than the critical density and the Universe would collapse.

As it turns out, the actual density is about 30 percent of the critical density. But if you extrapolate back in time, a 30 percent of critical density today translates into a 99.999999999999 percent of critical density one second after the Big Bang. This is amazingly close to 100 percent; in fact, one part in a million billion according to British cosmologist Sir Martin Rees.

Here is the amazing fine-tuning. If the density immediately after the Big Bang had been only 99.9 percent of critical, without all the other decimal-place nines, the density today would be many orders of magnitude less. This would have the consequence that the Universe would be expanding too fast for stars and galaxies to form.

And had it been just a fraction of a percent greater than 100 percent of the critical density at the very beginning, the Universe would have collapsed long ago.

Thus we have the situation that if the overall density of matter in the Universe had been higher or lower than it was at the very beginning, and by an utterly infinitesimal percentage, we would either have a lifeless Universe with black holes instead of stars, or else nothing but a tenuous gas filling the Universe instead of stars and planets. A millionth of a millionth percent difference either way at the time of the Big Bang would have doomed the Universe one way or the other. That is an impressive fine-tuning.

THE DARK MATTER RATIO

As reported in *New Scientist* (Dec. 6, 2008), the fact that dark matter is five to six times more abundant than ordinary matter is of considerable significance. That ratio is conducive to the formation of galaxies—whose stars are likely to have planets. But because ordinary matter and dark matter "probably formed via radically different processes shortly after the Big Bang" there is no obvious reason why their ratios should be so close. Dark matter could just as well have outdone ordinary matter by a thousand to one...or a million to one. Chalk up another fortuitous coincidence conducive to the formation of life-bearing planetary surfaces.

THE EVEN BIGGER MYSTERY OF DARK ENERGY

An even bigger mystery guest than dark matter came to the table in 1998: dark energy, something completely different from dark matter.

For decades astronomers had been measuring the expansion of the Universe with ever greater precision. The standard question was: Would the Universe keep expanding forever in spite of the gravitational self-attraction of all the matter in the Universe, or would that attraction win out in the end and pull the Universe back together into a Big Bang in reverse—you might say, a Big Crunch?

But no one seriously considered what the huge telescopes methodically measuring spectra of exploding stars, so-called supernovae, would show: that far from slowing down due to the gravitational self-attraction of matter, something was forcing the expansion of the Universe to accelerate, to speed up. That something is called dark energy. Like dark matter, we can't see it. But whereas dark matter is some unknown stuff, it still obeys the law of gravity. Dark energy is double the mystery. Not only do we not know what it is, we also do not know how it manages to defy the law of gravity by acting to push things apart. It acts like anti-gravity. And to top it off, the amount of dark energy comprises 70 percent of the Universe.

A minor increase in the amount of dark energy would have blown the Universe into a massive expansion without stars and planets. Things could have been very unfriendly for life.

QUANTUM CLUMPS

If the Big Bang had left the Universe in a smooth and uniform state of expansion, the Universe today would contain dark matter and rarefied hydrogen and helium gas with the density cited previously: about one atom of gas in a volume the size of a closet. But there would be no stars, no galaxies, no planets, and no other heavier elements.

Fortunately, for some reason, the aftermath of the Big Bang was not a perfectly uniform Universe. Small clumpiness that began as quantum fluctuations occurred, whose effects were magnified by gravity. But if this clumpiness had been greater or lesser by a factor of 10, the Universe would not have become a hospitable place for life.

Had it been 10 times more clumpy we would have a Universe filled with enormous black holes, containing the mass of an entire galaxy or more. Had it been 10 times less, galaxies would have had a difficult time forming at all. Stars would be further apart, and thus the heavy elements created in a first generation of stars—especially the carbon and oxygen essential for life—would be far less likely to condense into second- and third-generation stars—like our Sun—and simultaneously provide the raw material for the formation of planetary systems.

THE CHEMISTRY OF LIFE: CARBON AND OXYGEN

All life as we know it is based on carbon. Where does carbon come from? It is formed in the more massive stars that continue their nuclear reactions past the hydrogen-into-helium stage, and ultimately spew heavy elements back into the Universe when they end their lives in supernova explosions. The steps are hydrogen into helium, then helium into beryllium, and then helium plus beryllium into carbon. But beryllium is very unstable and quickly decays, so that last step should hardly ever occur...except for the fact that nature has provided a curious energy resonance that makes the reaction happen so quickly that carbon is formed before the beryllium can decay. That's why we have carbon in the Universe, and that's the key ingredient for life.

This leads to another fortuitous circumstance of the opposite sort. A similar resonance might reasonably be expected to exist leading to carbon quickly reacting to form oxygen, leaving no carbon behind. But such a resonance does not exist. Nature conspires to form some oxygen in massive stars, but not enough to wipe out the critical carbon. The end result is that we get just the right amount of both carbon and oxygen, and both are the essential elements for life.

THAT ORDINARY EXTRAORDINARY LIQUID: WATER

Even ordinary water has some odd properties that are crucial for life. Its boiling point is about 250 degrees Fahrenheit higher than that of comparable liquids. This allows it to act as a liquid in a range of temperatures conducive to biological structure.

Its freezing properties are also fortuitous. As science journalist Robert Matthews wrote in the British magazine *New Scientist*:

The fact that solid water—Ice—defies convention by being less dense than its liquid state has stopped the oceans from freezing solid from the bottom up and killing all marine life.

The ice cubes floating in your drink, rather than sinking to the bottom, are yet another reminder that the laws of the Universe are rather special.

Even more curious is the fact that zero-point energy stretches the bonds between hydrogen and oxygen in the water molecule in just the right way to allow the hydrogen atoms to link up with neighboring molecules more easily. (The zero-point energy is the underlying sea of energy due to quantum fluctuations, see *www.calphysics.org/zpe.html* or *The God Theory*.) Felix Franks of Cambridge University makes the point that swapping the hydrogen with its heavier isotope deuterium results in a liquid—heavy water—that is chemically identical, yet poisonous to all but the most primitive organisms. As Franks says: "The only difference is in the zero-point energy."

Without overinterpreting, it is interesting that zero-point energy may indirectly be involved in biology via its role in stretching the hydrogen bond in water.

WHICH IS HEAVIER? NEUTRON OR PROTON

In an article in *New Scientist*, Paul Davies points out that it matters a great deal that the neutron is 0.1 percent heavier than the proton. If it were the other way around, all protons that resulted from the Big Bang would long since have changed into neutrons, and this would preclude the formation of atoms. And without atoms there would be no Universe as we know it. As it is, neutrons are stable when they are part of an atomic nucleus, but decay quickly into protons, electrons, and neutrinos when they are free. But it takes a permanently stable proton to have led to the formation of stars and other matter.

WHAT HAPPENED TO ALL THE ANTI-MATTER?

Every fundamental particle of matter has an equal and opposite twin of antimatter. The positron is a positively charged electron. An anti-proton is a negatively charged proton made up of anti-quarks. It is in principle perfectly possible to have antimatter atoms of all the elements. Planets and stars made of antimatter would be just like planets and stars made of ordinary matter. There is no reason we could not have anti-people. When the Universe was created in the Big Bang, there should have been an equal amount of matter and antimatter created. The problem is that matter and antimatter immediately and completely destroy each other on contact, resulting in a burst of energy. For that reason we would not have a life-friendly universe, or any universe at all, if matter and antimatter had been created in equal amounts. We would have a Universe of all energy and no matter.

We also know that the stars and galaxies we see in the Universe must also be made of matter, rather than antimatter, because there are hydrogen atoms and other gases everywhere in space, and if half of that were antimatter there would be constant collisions between matter and anti-matter and astronomers would see annihilation signatures.

It is possible to infer from our knowledge of the Big Bang that for every 30,000,000 particles made of antimatter, there must have been 30,000,001 particles of matter. On average the 30,000,000 matter-antimatter pairs completely annihilated each other, leaving on average one particle of ordinary matter. It is that leftover one out of 30,000,000 out of which our Universe is made. Why this amazing almost but not complete cancellation? No one knows.

WHAT TO MAKE OF THIS

I propose that these fortuitous "just right" laws of nature point to a creator. Arguments for the existence of a creator based on the apparent complex design of things, both animate and inanimate, go far back, no doubt into prehistory. Today that goes by the name Intelligent Design, a cause being promoted nowadays with a good deal of political motivation behind it. But from astrophysics to biology we have discovered adequate natural causes for the rich variety of things on this planet and in the cosmos (given the right laws of nature to begin with).

Darwinian evolution has impressive explanatory power. Whether examples of so-called irreducible complexity—certain biological systems that appear too complex to have evolved from simpler predecessors while also too complex to have arisen naturally through chance mutations—prove to be temporary distractions or fatal flaws in evolution is not an issue that will be considered here. The question is whether the fundamental properties of the Universe itself, the laws of physics, manifest some specialness whose result is the existence of life, and perhaps even whose *purpose* is the existence of life.

The noteworthiness of the special properties discussed here is not in dispute. Carl Sagan alluded to some of them, although they were not as well known at the time. Books are out by authors such as British cosmologist Sir Martin Rees (*Just Six Numbers: The Deep Forces That Shape the Universe*) and Stanford physicist Leonard Susskind (*The Cosmic Landscape: String Theory and the Illusion of Intelligent Design*) that take these fortuitous properties as well established.

The extent to which scientists take these fortuitous properties seriously can perhaps be gauged by what they are willing to postulate in order to make sense of them. That ranges from the inferred existence of a huge number of other undetectable universes numbering one followed by 500 zeroes. To put that in perspective, the number of atoms in the Universe is only 10 followed by around 80 zeroes, essentially nothing by comparison.

And that's on the low side! The upper limit is a literally infinite number of other universes. What does that gain you?

Return to the Copernican Principle. It basically asserts that if something appears unique or special, that is almost certainly a fluke of observation. The Sun appears to be going around the Earth once a day. It sure looks that way and appeared to our ancestors as proof positive that the Earth was special, being at the center of the Universe. But in fact the Earth is rotating, and that's all there is to it.

The Copernican Principle explanation of our special Universe would go something like this: Yes, we and the Universe seem to be made for each other, but that does not mean our Universe was planned this way. It merely means that there must be a lot of other universes that are different from ours. In fact, there must be universes having all possible characteristics, a full range of properties, whatever they may be. But since those other universes are not hospitable to life as we know it, we could never find ourselves in one of those universes. We could only have originated in this universe, and that's why we find ourselves here.

It is a logical argument. But you are forced to accept the pre-existence of laws or fields of some kind. Quantum fluctuations, often taken as the origin of our universe, cannot happen without quantum laws.

The assumption of a huge number, perhaps even an infinite number, of other undetectable universes is also a weighty requirement.

And then there is the personal problem. If universes arise at random, then there is no ultimate purpose in our lives. This argument can be attacked as irrelevant. If that's how it is, then that's how it is: accept it and move on.

There is a purpose for our lives, from my perspective, one that is completely consistent with everything that science has discovered about the universe and about life on Earth. This purpose includes the Big Bang, a 4.6-billion-year-old Earth, and Darwinian evolution. This perspective assumes that an infinite conscious intelligence pre-existed before the creation of physical matter. It does not seem possible to have a universe without the pre-existence of something. This something might be an ensemble of physical laws generating infinite random universes or it might be an infinite conscious intelligence. Present-day science cannot resolve this pre-existing something, and it seems that neither view is more rational than the other.

At first glance it might seem that one view is supported by evidence and the other is not. The accounts of the mystics and the meditative, prayerful, and sometimes spontaneous exceptional experiences of human beings throughout history provide experiential evidence for the existence of an infinite conscious intelligence. There appears to be zero evidence for random universes, although this is a popular scientific theory. Scientists fond of the random universe theory will reject the experiential type of evidence for an infinite conscious intelligence as merely subjective. This reduces the contest of views to a draw: zero on both sides.

The idea of an infinite conscious intelligence with infinite potential, whose ideas become the laws of physics of our Universe and others makes sense to me. The consciousness providing purpose can be called God, who transforms potential into experience and gives our universe a purpose. There is a vast difference between being able to do something and actually doing it. Making it happen, experiencing what it feels like, and savoring the sensations provide the difference between theory and practice. It is more satisfying to play the game than it is to theorize about the rules.

"…the universe begins to look more like a great thought than like a great machine" is what astrophysicist Sir James Jeans wrote in the 1930s about his observations. I proposed something along those lines in *The God Theory*, that the origin of matter, energy, the laws of nature in this Universe and all others that may exist, arise ultimately from consciousness. God desires to experience his potential. The life of every sentient being expresses God's ideas and abilities. What greater purpose could there be for each of us than to create an experience for God? Because we are the incarnations of God in the physical realm, God experiences the richness of his potential through us.

Ironically one of the biggest challenges that this metaphysical view faces is the problem of religion, with its oftentimes pathological depictions of God, a small-minded God hobbled by not necessarily the best of human characteristics.

There has to be a better conception of God...and there is.

4

THE PERENNIAL PHILOSOPHY

Best-sellers have appeared recently that skewer religion: *The God Delusion* by Richard Dawkins; *Letter to a Christian Nation* by Sam Harris; *God: The Failed Hypothesis: How Science Shows That God Does Not Exist* by Victor Stenger; and *God Is Not Great: How Religion Poisons Everything* by Christopher Hitchins.

These are very angry books, and they have sold well. They make many valid points. Consider the following quote from the Bible that Harris cites:

"If a man discovers on his wedding night that his bride is not a virgin, he must stone her to death on her father's doorstep." (Deuteronomy 22:13)

Or let this one sink in:

"If your brother...or your son, or your daughter, or your wife, or your friend who is as your own soul, entices you secretly, saying, 'Let us go and serve other gods,'... you shall not yield to him, nor shall your eye pity him, nor shall you spare him, nor shall you conceal him; but you shall kill him...you shall stone him to death...." *(Deuteronomy 13:6)*

And one more for good measure:

"As you approach a city to fight against it, first offer it a truce. If it accepts the truce and opens its gates to you, then all its people shall become your servants. But if it refuses and will not make peace with you, you must besiege it. When the Lord your God has given it to you, kill every male in the city; but you may keep for yourselves all the women, children, cattle and booty. These instructions apply only to the distant cities, not to those in the promised land itself. For in the cities within the boundaries of the promised land itself you are to save no one; destroy every living thing." Deuteronomy (9:3)

I am in total sympathy with Harris's view that a God who would make such laws is a reprehensible sociopath and not the kind of entity that I could conceivably worship, much less respect. And such views are not safely confined to the biblical past: Witness the barbaric slaughter of innocents in the Middle East today motivated by the expectation of a paradisical reward for the most horrendous atrocities. This is absolute craziness. I thus found myself, to my own surprise, cheering for Harris's clear and compelling exposé of religious lunacy and the suffering it is causing. Harris is absolutely correct in faulting religion for intolerance, violence, and hatred, things that are the exact opposite of spirituality.

But the human misuse of religion and the existence of God are two very different things.

Just as our understanding of nature has evolved, so too should our understanding of God. But if so, where is that knowledge to come from? I suggest that it has been part of human culture and history from ancient times.

As Eckhart Tolle writes in his *A New Earth*:

And yet… in spite of all the insane deeds perpetrated in the name of religion, the Truth to which they point still shines at their core. It still shines, however dimly, through layers upon layers of distortion and misinterpretation.

THE PERENNIAL PHILOSOPHY

Within all religions there lies a mystical stream, a repository of wisdom based on mankind's contact with something other than physical reality. It goes by the name of *the Perennial Philosophy*, a phrase coined by Agostino Steuco, an Italian Old Testament scholar and Catholic bishop, in a book he wrote in 1540: *De Perenni Philosophia Libri X*. He presented the ideas in the context of Christianity. His book was even dedicated to Pope Paul III and attempted to show

that many of the ideas propounded by sages and philosophers of antiquity were in harmony with Catholic teachings.

The Perennial Philosophy was later made famous in a
non-sectarian context by Gottfried Leibnitz, the 18th-century
mathematical genius who discovered the binary number system, the basis of modern computer operation. (He also discovered calculus independently of Newton. Beyond mathematics he wrote so much that there is as yet no compendium
of all his writing...such as his tens of thousands of letters.
He was a busy man.)

The Perennial Philosophy is based on the experience of
people throughout history and from many different cultures
with respect to the nature of reality, the self, and the meaning and purpose of existence. It suggests universal principles
underlying the world's many different religions.

The definitive modern overview is the book *The Perennial
Philosophy* published in 1945 by Aldous Huxley. Physicist
Erwin Schroedinger, one of the founders of quantum mechanics responsible for the famous wave equation at the
heart of the new physics had this to say about Huxley's book.

*Ten years ago, Aldous Huxley published a precious
volume which he called The Perennial Philosophy and
which is an anthology from the mystics of the most
various periods and the most various peoples. Open it
where you will and you find many beautiful utterances
of a similar kind. You are struck by the miraculous
agreement between humans of different race, different
religion, knowing nothing about each other's existence,
separated by centuries and millennia, and by the greatest distances that there are on the globe.* (What is Life,
1967)

Three essential tenets of the Perennial Philosophy are:

1. The physical universe of matter is not the sole re-
    alty. Other non-physical realities exist which may
    contain other life-forms. Thus the material world
    is a shadow of a greater reality not directly per-
    ceivable by the physical senses. It is interesting
    that this concept is potentially compatible with
    string and M-theories that are at the forefront of
    modern physics, since those theories necessarily
    involve other dimensions that may have radically
    different sets of laws.
2. Our human nature has both a material side sub-
    ject to physical laws, birth, and death, as well as a
    non-material immortal spirit or soul, which is ac-
    tually the more essential side because it is made
    of the same stuff as the ultimate source, which is
    generally regarded as God.
3. All humans possess a capacity to intuitively per-
    ceive the true multifaceted nature of ourselves
    and the greater reality. Attuning to this percep-
    tion is an essential goal of human life, but un-
    fortunately is generally dormant in most human
    beings (that being the reason that the world is in
    such a sad state).

The essentials of Perennial Philosophy were written
down more than 25 centuries ago in India and are to be
found in the mystical streams of all religions, including
Christianity.

REQUISITE CONDITIONS

But if we have such ability, why is it dormant? It appears
that to activate the power to directly and immediately ap-
prehend this greater reality certain conditions are required:

making oneself loving, pure of heart, and poor in spirit. The latter rather quaint phrase "poor in spirit" can be defined as being devoid of pride, envy, and lust while appreciating, respecting, and making good use of the things we are "blessed" with, especially if they can be used to benefit others. It means not having undue attachment to things, not basing our identity on our possessions.

Why should such conditions be necessary? As Huxley writes: "Why should this be so? We do not know. It is just one of those facts which we have to accept, whether we like them or not and however implausible and unlikely they may seem."

Western civilization today being more obsessed than ever with the creation and acquisition of wealth and the things money can buy, it is little wonder that the ability to see beyond our physical realm is widely dormant and officially even unrecognized by mainstream society.

The requirements of being loving, pure of heart, and poor in spirit in order to directly tap into spiritual information rather immediately also explains why all too many religious leaders are not even cognizant of spiritual facts, even though that should be their "line of business." If you preach hate against those not on your side, you will not satisfy the prerequisite of being loving. That is a sure obstacle to direct perception of a spiritual reality.

A pure heart is one that is free from contamination. Dislike, intolerance, or hatred of others leads to a heart that is not pure in that sense, and so yet another blinder is in place for those who would hate. And arguably a third strike comes about on the "poor in spirit" pitch, for the reason that the well-being of others, which is part of being poor in spirit, is not enhanced by hatred.

Intellectual pride would also be incompatible with the "poor in spirit" requirement. Indeed, even without falling into an excess of pride, I suspect that an overemphasis on the intellect alone would probably be a major obstacle...and might well explain why the author of this book does not, alas, have direct perception.

It is also the case that the mindset and openness to other realities that leads to the ability to perceive a non-physical reality is generally at odds with the scientific mentality. Although it is not impossible for a scientist to experience such things, the cards are stacked against it. This can lead to the glib conclusion on the part of scientists that the Perennial Philosophy is purely subjective imagination, and to some degree this is probably the majority opinion of modern scientists.

EDDINGTON AND EINSTEIN

Perhaps the most noteworthy exception in modern times is Sir Arthur Eddington. He is widely regarded as one of the greatest scientists of the early 20th century. In 1919, he led the eclipse expedition to Principe, an island off the coast of Africa, that made a crucial test of Einstein's General Theory of Relativity. This observation proved to be among the most important in the history of science. It provided the clinching evidence for one of the truly revolutionary ideas of all time: that space is curved, or more precisely, spacetime.

For over two centuries Newton's theory of gravity as a force operating in a flat space was a tremendous success. The orbits of the planets in the Solar System followed Newton's theory with amazing precision (apart from a minor discrepancy in the case of the planet Mercury).

A flat space is the one we ordinarily experience and think in terms of. It is defined by the property that parallel lines stay parallel no matter how far they stretch off into the distance. They always keep the same separation from each other. They never come together, they never diverge. This is the common-sense view we have of ordinary space and goes by the name of Euclidean geometry after the Greek philosopher and father of geometry, Euclid, who formulated geometry more than

2,000 years ago. Until the mid-19th century no one thought that any other geometry was even possible. But it was. Mathematicians such as the German Bernhard Riemann demonstrated the theoretical possibility of spaces whose dimensions are curved. In some of these geometries lines that are parallel intersect each other elsewhere.

In 1915 Einstein published a theory of gravity now known as the General Theory of Relativity. It is called that because it extends, and hence is more general than his earlier work on the laws of moving objects known as Special Relativity. In Einstein's theory, gravity is not a force at all. It is a manifestation of the curvature of space (to be precise, spacetime together).

Although the concepts underlying Newtonian gravity and Einsteinian gravity were as different as day and night, one being a force, the other a curvature of space itself, the differences between known observations was miniscule. As it turned out, the curvature of space could be directly measured…but only during an eclipse of the Sun. At such a time the curvature of space produced by the Sun should be measurable by looking at the positions of stars on either side of the Sun. They could only be seen in that position, though, when the brilliant light of the Sun was blocked out by the Moon during an eclipse. This is shown in Figure 5. The light from two stars in the sky is bent—because space itself is curved—when the Sun happens to lie in between the two light beams.

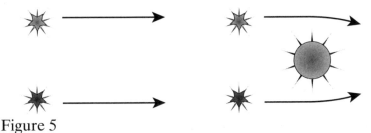

Figure 5

The idea was to take a precise photograph—on rigid glass plates—of the stars in a region of the sky where the Sun would be during an eclipse and to very carefully measure the stars in that field on a plate taken without the Sun present versus one taken when the Sun was present and the stars visible thanks to the eclipse. If Einstein's theory was correct, the stars nearest the Sun—nearest meaning adjacent in the sky, the actual distances from both the Earth and Sun would be enormous, but not relevant—would be slightly shifted from their normal pattern.

In 1915, when Einstein first published his theory, World War I was raging. It would go on for three more years. When it ended in 1918, British Astronomer Royal Sir Frank Dyson began preparing for the next available eclipse, on May 29, 1919, to test Einstein's theory. He recruited Arthur Eddington, Plumian Professor of Astronomy at Cambridge, to lead a scientific expedition into the path of the total eclipse. Dyson was close to Eddington because Eddington, as a Quaker and pacifist, had nearly been forced into conscientious objector labor during the War, but Dyson had arranged for a deferment, allowing the brilliant Eddington to continue his research. Apparently in return for this, Eddington had to agree to lead a trek to the island of Principe, off the coast of West Africa, near the center of the eclipse track where the duration would be the longest. A second team, led by Dr. A.C.D. Crommelin of the Royal Observatory at Greenwich would be dispatched to Sobral, not far from the port of Fortaleza in Brazil where the eclipse would show itself about an hour earlier but with somewhat shorter duration.

The maximum duration of a solar eclipse is seven and a half minutes. The eclipse on Principe would last five minutes and two seconds. Fortuitously the Sun would be seen against a field containing the rich Hyades cluster of stars. This would provide ample targets whose positions could be measured from plates taken during the eclipse and compared to plates taken months earlier or later when the same star field was visible at night.

Unfortunately as the date of the eclipse approached, things did not look promising. For most days leading up to the eclipse...it rained! As the eclipse began on May 29 clouds partially covered the Sun. Eddington and his assistant, a Mr. E.T. Cunningham, furiously exposed the large glass photographic plates. They managed to obtain 16 altogether, ranging in exposure from two to 20 seconds. But it was really only the final plate that showed fairly good images of five stars.

Most of the Sobral plates developed in Brazil did not look promising either. But some of the plates taken with a four-inch lens were only developed back in England. One of the plates showed good images of seven stars.

Einstein's theory predicted that starlight grazing the surface of the Sun would be deflected by 1.75 seconds of arc (less than the width of a human hair held at arm's length). The analysis Eddington and his colleagues carried out in England showed a deflection of 1.61 seconds of arc from the Principe plate and 1.98 seconds of arc from the Sobral plate, nicely bracketing the Einstein prediction.

The final results were presented by Sir Frank Dyson at a meeting of the prestigious Royal Society of London. From there the news quickly telegraphed around the world. The *New York Times*, in the style of the day, had headlines and subheadlines on the front page of November 10, 1919.

LIGHTS ALL ASKEW IN THE HEAVENS

Men of Science More or Less Agog Over Results of Eclipse Observations.

EINSTEIN THEORY TRIUMPHS

Stars Not Where They Seemed or Were Calculated to be, but Nobody Need Worry.

A BOOK FOR 12 WISE MEN

No More in All the World Could Comprehend It, Said Einstein When His Daring Publishers Accepted It.

With respect to the headline about this being a "book for 12 wise men," a kind of urban legend, which I myself heard as a graduate student, was that Eddington was asked by a reporter whether it was true that only three men understood relativity. Eddington is said to have replied: "I can't think of who the third one would be."

Einstein achieved instant fame around the world when the eclipse measurement story came out in the *New York Times* and elsewhere. Being the leader of the observing team, Eddington would have achieved considerable fame from this alone. But it is for good reason that Subramanyan Chandrasekhar, a Nobel-prize–winning astrophysicist himself of legendary stature, published a book in 1982 on the hundredth anniversary of Eddington's birth entitled: *Eddington: The Most Distinguished Astrophysicist of his Time.* For indeed, after proving Einstein's General Relativity to be correct, Eddington took on the daunting task in 1923 of writing the first textbook thoroughly explaining and developing Einstein's theory in 260 pages of dense tensor calculus (which I had the mixed pleasure of using myself decades later as a graduate student). And if that was not enough, only three years after that, he published the landmark *The Internal Constitution of the Stars* which effectively created the field of study of the structure and evolution of stars.

Eddington was well rewarded for this hard work and genius. In the 1930s and 1940s his name was a household word in the English-speaking world thanks to the numerous popular articles he wrote bringing astronomy to the general public, and his awards included five medals; a crater on the moon and an asteroid named for him; presidency of the Royal Astronomical Society and later of the International Astronomical Union; and of course that ultimate British mark of distinction: a knighthood.

EDDINGTON AND HIS INNER LIGHT

Eddington spent his life trying to bring together science and spirituality. As discussed by astronomer Alan Batten a few years ago in the *Quarterly Journal of the Royal Astronomical Society*: "He (Eddington) was trying to reconcile, or even unite, the two most important things in his life: the excitement of scientific research and the profundity of his own mystical experience. In each realm alike, he saw himself as a seeker led by an 'Inner Light.'"

Batten claims that it is hard to tell from Eddington's writings which was more important to him: his scientific research or his spiritual experiences. It is evident from his writings that he had some sorts of personal mystical experiences. Eddington saw himself primarily as a seeker. About this seeking he wrote:

We seek the truth: but if some voice told us that a few years more would see the end of our journey, that the clouds of uncertainty would be dispersed, and that we should perceive the whole truth about the physical Universe, the tidings would by no means be joyful. In science as in religion the truth shines ahead as a beacon showing us the path; we do not ask to attain it; it is better far that we be permitted to seek. (Science and the Unseen World, *1929)*

He came to the conclusion that "ultimate reality" was spiritual in nature and that the laws of nature were the creation of spirit or mind. His view was that particles and quanta were only manifestations in the scientific world of some deeper, mainly inscrutable reality.

He expressed belief in a personal God and placed a high value on "mystical religion." But in fact what he termed "religion" was essentially a non-sectarian spirituality. Eddington's Quaker religion after all has no creed, no dogma, not even any paid clergy or formal service. There is thus hardly any difference between the "religion of Quakerism" and simply being spiritual but areligious.

Eddington was criticised by the professional philosophers of the time on the grounds that his metaphysical writings were inconsistent, obscure, or even logically flawed. Examined from a rigorous academic point of view, such criticisms could be more or less valid. Remember, though, that unlike Eddington's science, which was of paramount rigor and precision, his metaphysical writings were of a popular nature, not intended for scholarly examination and dissection.

But this kind of criticism from professional philosophers actually illustrates the point Aldous Huxley makes in his introduction to *The Perennial Philosophy*. Addressing the requisite conditions for direct experience of "higher realities"—making oneself loving, pure of heart, and poor in spirit—he notes that: "In regard to few professional philosophers and men of letters is there any evidence that they did very much in the way of fulfilling the necessary conditions of direct spiritual knowledge."

Eddington appears to have been the sort of individual who to some extent did fulfill those conditions and thus actually tapped a direct mystical source: his "inner light," which was the basis of what he tried to convey. He drew insights from his experiences, and that these lacked the requirements of philosophical rigor says more about the sterility of that rigor than about any failing on Eddington's part. The criticism by one major philosopher that Eddington's philosophy was a generation out of date with the trend in philosophical thinking is telling. The Perennial Philosophy had better *not* change from one generation to another. The criticism of Eddington by the philosophers reinforces Huxley's point.

Eddington was still at the height of his career when he published *Science and the Unseen World* in 1929. In it he wrote:

Are we, in pursuing the mystical outlook, facing the hard facts of experience? Surely we are. I think that those who would wish to take cognisance of nothing but the measurements of the scientific world made by our sense-organs are shirking one of the most immediate facts of experience, namely that consciousness is not wholly, nor even primarily a device for receiving sense-impressions.

It was a bold thing to do, to publicly express the view that there is another realm, or perhaps more likely other realms, of reality beyond the physical universe.

THE UNIVERSE BEGINS TO LOOK MORE LIKE A GREAT THOUGHT THAN LIKE A GREAT MACHINE

Britain's two best known astronomers in the 1930s and 1940s were Eddington and Sir James Jeans. Together they gave Britain a prominent position in cosmology—the study of the nature of the Universe—which still persists today. Jeans' contributions to astrophysics were in the areas of quantum theory, electromagnetic radiation, and the evolution of stars.

Jeans was five years older than Eddington and retired from active research in 1929 at the young age of 54. From that point on he became a popularizer of astronomy both in terms of scientific discovery and philosophical implications. Jeans and Eddington thereby acquired substantial influence as popular interpreters of the nature of the Universe, and even though they did not collaborate, their parallel writings with similar perspectives wound up reinforcing each other. They held similar views with respect to the existence of a non-physical reality, Eddington using the term "spiritual" and Jeans using the term "mental" but both meaning approximately the same thing.

Their writings came across as showing that new 20th-century discoveries in physics and astrophysics were much more supportive of a belief in God than the 19th-century views dominated by Darwin's evolution and Newton's physics. Taken together classical Newtonian physics and evolution implied that human beings are nothing more than machines originating by chance and devoid even of free will. This thankfully changes entirely in light of 20th-century quantum physics, but the best scientific knowledge of the 19th century painted a bleak picture indeed of human nature.

A strict interpretation of Newton's physics implies that free will is an illusion, because in the mechanistic view of matter, every single thing that happens now is based on what happened previously, down to the most minute level. From that perspective even our own actions, every breath we take or word we utter, is preordained from the configuration of everything that went before. In that sense a Mozart symphony could be traced back to the dust of the ancient earth: every note could have been predicted a billion years ago by a super intelligence capable of taking into account where every atom in the universe was located and with what velocity it was moving at any given instant. Even T.H. Huxley, the hard-nosed naturalist known as Darwin's bulldog for his aggressive defense of Darwin's theory of evolution in the 1860s—and, ironically, grandfather of Aldous Huxley— alluded to the "19th century nightmare" of complete determinism. As astronomer Alan Batten writes in his article on Eddington, "If the motions of our bodies are determined by all that has gone before, the questions of whether we are determined by our genes, our upbringing and environment, or even the grace of God, are all academic."

With the coming of quantum mechanics and its inherent uncertainty, free will was no longer in blatant contradiction of physics. Both Eddington and Jeans had strong opinions about the existence of free will, and their views gave the impression that science and spirituality were compatible after all.

Unlike Eddington, Jeans seems not to have been a mystic in the experiential sense. He was greatly influenced by quantum ideas. In his book, *The Mysterious Universe*, Jeans wrote:

Again we may think of the laws to which phenomena conform...the laws of nature, as the laws of thought of a universal mind...the universe begins to look more like a great thought than like a great machine. Mind no longer appears as an accidental intruder into the realm of matter; we are beginning to suspect that we ought rather to hail it as the creator and governor of the realm of matter.

Although their scientific careers are now many decades in the past, Eddington and Jeans were certainly scientists in the modern sense. I imagine both would be perfectly capable of getting up to speed today and contributing to the forefront of science because the basic concepts have not changed that much. General Relativity still governs the Universe and quantum physics has been greatly elaborated and developed but is still fundamentally the same theory developed in the Eddington-Jeans era. Their metaphysical views cannot be dismissed on the grounds that they did not sufficiently understand or appreciate the scientific worldview.

And as to the criticisms by the philosophers that neither man was *philosophically au courant*, I would, in the case of Eddington, take his direct mystical experience as a better indicator of true knowledge than the scholarly logic of the professionals.

The discovery that our universe appears to be finely tuned would almost certainly have been welcome news—but probably not a great surprise—to Sir Arthur Eddington and Sir James Jeans.

5

THOU
ART
THAT

The most important concept of the Perennial Philosophy can be stated simply as "Thou art that." It is the most important statement in the ancient spiritual tradition that grew up in India called Vedanta. In the nomenclature of Vedanta, God is called Brahman and our own spiritual self is called Atman. The "thou art that" statement means that we (Atman) are of the same stuff as God (Brahman).

It is important not to get sidetracked by this terminology or its cultural connotations. I put no credence whatsoever in the vast Hindu pantheon of deities and entities—numbering over 300 million!—that has grown up over the ages. No monkey gods for me! Those superstitious beliefs are just a distraction from an essential core truth. It is just that this religious tradition is where some of the most ancient ideas that we can still access today may be found. The central idea of Vedanta is the identity of Atman with Brahman. The Christian equivalent of Atman is sometimes called "the Christ within," but I will call Atman simply the soul.

A LITTLE THEOLOGY

Brahman is said to be the sole reality, a transcendent intelligence beyond all attributes: unchanging, infinite, immanent; the Divine Ground of all matter, energy, time, space, being, and everything in this Universe and whatever others there may be.

I equate Brahman with the Godhead in Christian mystical terminology, and Ein-Sof in Kaballah. Godhead, Ein-Sof, and Brahman I thus take to be different names for the same infinite intelligence. Thomas Aquinas had a Latin name for the Godhead: Deus Absconditus, the hidden God. The appropriateness of "hidden" relative to a real and personal God the Creator will become clear.

The distinction between Godhead and God the Creator is subtle, but important. The Godhead is unmanifest. Beyond space, beyond time, beyond any attributes: simultaneously greater than infinity and less than zero. When the Godhead chooses to create a universe, such as ours, he/she sends forth a part of himself to be both the Creator and the created. In the Vedantic tradition Brahman awakes from his slumber and breathes out a creation—figuratively speaking. At the conclusion of that creation—which in the case of our Universe would be billions of years—all things return to Brahman because they always have been nothing other than part of him all along, and he sleeps again...figuratively speaking.

Imagine a successful but very private novelist: call him Richard Wordsworth, who writes under the pen name of T.S. Thompson. No one knows a thing about Wordsworth. If you Googled him you would find nothing and no one would even know he exists. But millions read the novels of T.S. Thompson. It is publicly known that Thompson is a pen name, but who it refers to is a mystery. When Wordsworth is inspired to create, he emerges as T.S. Thompson and creates a new reality in his novel. Thompson is the creative public face of Wordsworth. You might even say that the imaginary Thompson was the creator of the novel, and this is true insofar as Wordsworth assumes the identity of Thompson in order to successfully create. But the real person is the hidden Wordsworth.

How can the Brahman-Ein-Sof-Godhead exist out of space and time and yet bring creations to life? How can some intelligence that is absolute and perfect blissful tranquility also be the dynamic source of creation? How do you go from state A to state B without time? I don't pretend to know. It is a mystery. But the fact is that this apparently self-contradictory state has been experienced directly by many men and women throughout history in the mystical experience. Naturally none are able to adequately translate this back into ordinary language. Words do not exist. They know for certain that in that otherworldly state they *knew*, but can no longer express it. How do you explain the color red to someone born blind? All things begin with points of reference and then you combine and compare and contrast them to communicate an idea. But where there is no shared point of reference, description becomes impossible.

Like novelist Thompson emerging in public from reclu-
sive Wordsworth, God the Creator is a manifestation of the
Godhead, not a separate being. I will simply use the term
God for both aspects.

Consider the following from *The Crest Jewel of Wisdom*,
attributed to the ancient Indian sage Sankara.

---

*The wise man is one who understands that the essence
of Brahman and of Atman is pure consciousness, and
who realizes their absolute identity.*

That statement is telling us two very important things:
first, that consciousness is the root of everything, because
it is the essence of both God and ourselves, and secondly
that the consciousness of God and our own consciousness
are identical.

The 13th-century Sufi mystic Ibn Arabi wrote:

---

*When the mystery of the oneness of the soul and the
Divine is revealed to you, you will understand that you
are not other than God.... For when you know yourself,
your sense of a limited identity vanishes, and you know
that you and God are one and the same.*

And again from the Vedanta:

---

*He is the immutable Foundation of all that exists; those
souls who realize Him as their very own Self are freed
forever from the need for rebirth. When that Lord, who
pervades all the worlds everywhere, gave birth to the*

first motion, He manifested Himself as creation. It is He alone who is born in this world. He lives as all beings; it is only Him everywhere.... He takes the form of the limited soul, appearing to be bound; but, in fact, He is forever free. Brahman appears as Creator, and also as the limited soul. He is the Power that creates the appearance of the world. Yet He remains unlimited and unaffected by these appearances. When one knows that Brahman, then that soul becomes free. The forms of the world change, like clouds in the sky; but Brahman, the Lord, remains One and unchanged. He is the Ruler of all worlds and all souls. Through meditation on Him, and communion with Him, He becomes known...and one therefore becomes freed from illusion. (Svetasvatara Upanishad)

CONSCIOUSNESS AND CAUSES

The concept that consciousness is primary is at odds with the modern scientific perspective that somehow consciousness arises out of matter in some kind of evolutionary process. In *The God Delusion* Dawkins advocates that:

...any creative intelligence, of sufficient complexity to design anything, comes into existence only as the end product of an extended process of gradual evolution. Creative intelligences, being evolved, necessarily arrive late in the universe, and therefore cannot be responsible for designing it.

What Dawkins fails to take into consideration is that the process of evolution, which in his view can result after some lengthy period in a creative intelligence, itself requires some antecedent cause. Where did laws resulting in evolution come from? As Shakespeare wrote, "Nothing will come of nothing." Aristotle's notion of a primary cause is still valid. At some initial point we are logically forced to accept something as just preexising, itself an uncaused cause. Our choice is what kind of primary cause we are willing to accept as such. At a minimum the Dawkins argument would require the preexistence of some kind of laws.

The Perennial Philosophy maintains that there exists an uncaused God, whose consciousness is then the cause of everything that follows.

The first-century Jewish philosopher Philo of Alexandria wrote:

God is high above place and time…. He is contained by nothing, but transcends all. But, though transcending what He has made, nonetheless, He fills the universe with Himself.

This is consistent with Jeans's remark that the Universe looks more like a great thought than like a great machine, and in the Perennial Philosophy that is precisely what the Universe is: the conscious thought of an intelligence that simply *is*, without beginning, without end, beyond space and time and without any origin or cause beyond itself.

The strongly held view of quantum founder Erwin Schroedinger was that there is only one consciousness pervading the Universe and that each of us is like a window through which that consciousness manifests itself. In his writings he quotes the 13th-century mystic Aziz Nasafi.

On the death of any living creature the spirit returns to the spiritual world, the body to the bodily world. In this however only the bodies are subject to change. The spiritual world is one single spirit who stands like unto a light behind the bodily world and who, when any single creature comes into being, shines through it as through a window. According to the kind and size of the window less or more light enters the world. The light itself however remains unchanged. (What is Life, 1967)

BEGINNING OF TIME

Stephen Hawking and his collaborator James Hartle argued that owing to the fact that space and time are intermingled in relativity theory, there may be a way to go back to a moment in time that has no prior moment. Imagine traveling north on the Earth. The farthest north we can go is to the North Pole. Once there, no matter what direction we take, we will be going south. Hawking and Hartle showed that space and time can curve into each other, under conditions like the Big Bang, so that as you travel farther and farther back in time there comes a time when no matter what you do you wind up curving back into a forward trajectory in time.

If true, this would be a very neat way to sidestep the endless question of what happened before the Big Bang. In the Hawking-Hartle view there is in effect a first moment, one that at least in principle you could go back to, but beyond which you cannot go, just like trying to go further north beyond the North Pole. There is a very definite North Pole at which there is no further going north possible.

I am wholeheartedly in agreement that this would be a neat way to establish a definite moment of beginning for the Universe, and as far as the Universe is concerned there simply would be no prior time. Time began with the Big Bang. Time and the Universe came together in one package deal. This, by the way, is a view propounded by St. Augustine almost 2,000 years ago.

But I contend that the Hawking-Hartle view is not the same as solving the causation argument. What made the Universe and time itself appear? Now, of course, the fact of the matter is that no one, no philosopher, no scientist, no theologian, not the author of this book, knows how causation might operate when there is no time to operate in. My contention and that of the Perennial Philosophy is that the cause of the Universe is God. Again, from the *Crest-Jewel of Wisdom*:

> *Brahman has neither name nor form, transcends merit and demerit, is beyond time, space ,and the objects of sense perception.*
> *Pure, absolute and eternal Reality—such is Brahman.*
> *Though one, Brahman is the cause of the many.*
> *There is no other cause. And yet Brahman is independent of the law of causation.*
> *It has ordained that all things should be limited, but is itself unlimited, infinite.*

The idea that our consciousness is absolutely identical with God's is perhaps harder to take seriously. After all, we human beings are far from any reasonable attributes of God. In what sense might we have an essence which is the same as the essence of God? The next chapter proposes a way in which this makes sense.

MEISTER ECKHART

These ideas, while stated previously in mainly Vedantic terms, are not unique to that tradition. One of the most influential mystics in Christianity was Eckhart von Hochheim, better known as Meister Eckhart (1260–1327). *Meister* is simply the German word for "master," a title he acquired for his academic studies in Paris. Eckhart was a prominent member of the Dominican Order, but in fact his teachings were quite novel, ultimately leading to a charge of heresy. Central themes of Eckhart's metaphysics are the "fertility" of God, referring to his outpouring of love to launch creation, and God's presence in the soul of human beings. Indeed he too taught that we and God are ultimately the same.

As the soul becomes more pure and bare and poor, and possesses less of created things, and is emptied of all things that are not God, it receives God more purely, and is more completely in Him; and it truly becomes one with God, and it looks into God and God into it, face to face as it were; two images transformed into one.... Some simple people think that they will see God as if He were standing there and they here. It is not so. God and I, we are one.... By the living God, it is true that there is no distinction!

He also distinguished God as creator from the ultimate, absolute, and unmanifest Godhead.

The 19th-century German philosopher Arthur Schopenhauer wrote that Meister Eckhart and the Buddha taught the same thing, although Eckhart was "obliged to clothe them in the garment of Christian myth." Other scholars have drawn similar parallels between Eckhart's metaphysics and Buddhism.

> *God is not only a Father of all good things, as being their First Cause and Creator, but He is also their Mother, since He remains with the creatures which have from Him their being and existence, and maintains them continually in their being. If God did not abide with and in the creatures, they must necessarily have fallen back, so soon as they were created, into the nothingness out of which they were created. All creatures are a pure nothing. I don't say they are insignificant or a something: they are absolute nothing. Whatever hasn't essence does not exist. No creature has essence, because the essence of all is in the presence of God. If God withdrew from the creatures for just one moment, they would disappear to nothing.*

FINDING GOD WITHIN

But if indeed we are one with God, that answers the question of where to look for God: inside ourselves. Atman is the inmost essence of our being, and because it is one with Brahman, God in effect resides in us...and even in Prof. Dawkins, whether he likes it or not.

In his book *Science and the Unseen World*, Eddington remarks that astronomers tend to be put off when confronted by religious folk with the psalm: "The heavens declare the glory of God." I can fully appreciate why one would be sorely temped to reply, "No, the heavens declare the marvels of astrophysics."

But then Eddington goes on to say that there is a passage that does come near to his own sympathies:

And behold the Lord passed by, and a great and strong wind rent the mountains, and brake in pieces the rocks before the Lord; but the Lord was not in the wind. And after the wind an earthquake; but the Lord was not in the earthquake. And after the earthquake a fire; but the Lord was not in the fire. And after the fire a still small voice…and behold there came a voice unto him, and said, What doest thou here, Elijah?

It was the still small voice inside which Eddington often heard and to which he attributed significance.

And again reaffirming the identity of Brahman and Atman together with the presence of God within, Meister Eckhart wrote:

I have maintained ere this and I still maintain that I already possess all that is granted to me in eternity. For God in the fullness of his Godhead dwells eternally in his image—the soul.

In the ancient Vedantic texts it is written:

In the beginning, there was Existence alone—One only, without a second. It, the One, thought to itself: "Let me be many, let me grow forth." Thus, out of Itself, It entered into every being. All that is, has itself in It alone. Of all things it is the subtle essence. It is the truth. It is the Self. And you are That.

THE MYSTICAL EXPERIENCE: "I AND THE FATHER ARE ONE"

The Godhead is neither mind nor matter, but a reality beyond rational comprehension that is eternal, omniscient, omnipresent, and which experiences itself as pure consciousness and bliss. It is the Spirit immanent in everything that seemingly exists in the Universe, including us. There is no difference between the source and the manifestation. So how can we know this? Because in the Mystical Experience that people have, that is what is directly experienced and becomes known in a way and at a level that transcends language, logic, and rational knowledge.

Spiritual nondualism, that our nature is ultimately identical with the transcendent consciousness behind all creation, is reported in the visions of all mystics. It is uniformly experienced by mystics from all religious traditions.

What I will call simply the Mystical Experience has been described this way (Swami Abhayananda, *The Divine Universe*):

That magical night, while sitting there before the fire in my dark cabin…I was privileged to see into the real nature of my self and all existence. When the veil of ignorance, which constitutes the ego, was lifted, it was revealed that my true, underlying identity is, and had always been, the one all-pervading Consciousness that is the Source and substratum of all that exists.

The soul, seeking God, scans the inner darkness, as though to discover another, as though awaiting something external to itself to make its presence known. But as the concentration focuses within, the mind becomes stilled, and suddenly the seeking soul awakes. No external has made its appearance; it is the soul itself, no longer soul, which knows itself to be the All, the One. Like a wave seeking the ocean, the seeker discovers that it is, itself, what it sought.

When God reveals Himself, He is not seen as something or someone apart. The soul is lifted up to identity with God, so that there is no longer a soul, but God Himself is revealed as one's own Self. That Self is eternal, beyond all manifestation, never affected by the ongoing drama of worldly experience. It masquerades as every being, all the while remaining purely Consciousness and perfect Bliss.

Those who have risen yet higher (or more inwardly) toward their Source have experienced themselves no longer as individual separate identities, but rather as ideational wave-forms on the one integral ocean of Cosmic Energy. They no longer identify with the composite of body, mind, and soul, but know themselves as having their real identity in the entire undivided ocean of creative Energy in and on which these temporary forms manifest. The conscious awareness focused on this clear vision of the subtler level of its own reality then moves forward, as one moving through a fog comes to a clearing where the fog is no more, to the ultimate and final level of subtlety, the Divine Source, the Unmanifest. Then, it knows the pure unqualified Consciousness that is the Father, prior even to the creative Power which acts as creator; and it knows, "I and the Father are one."

6

THE GOD THEORY

Petty, vindictive, sadomasochistic, genocidal…these are just four of the 16 adjectives Richard Dawkins uses to describe the God of the various scriptures, including but not limited to the Bible. And even Thomas Jefferson characterized the God widely depicted in his day as cruel, vindictive, capricious, and unjust.

A jealous God who hates. A God who demands stoning women to death. A God who supplies virgins in paradise to deranged bombers for incinerating innocent women and children in a crowded market place. That God I would wholeheartedly agree would be a foul being worthy of contempt rather than praise, a toss-up with the devil for the number-one villain of the Universe.

But this is not the God of the Perennial Philosophy. An adulation-hungry God who would require those things could not possibly be "big" enough, in a visionary and a moral sense, to create with his thoughts a Universe as grand as ours. The God I proposed in my book *The God Theory*, and which I discuss here, is a very different God from the one so many people invoke to justify their own hatreds and nightmares.

GOD AND GODHEAD

As discussed in the previous chapter, the Perennial Philosophy advocates a distinction between God and Godhead. At first glance this might seem like frivolous theological hair-splitting, a practice not unknown to the theology business. But there is an important distinction to be drawn as reported by those who have had the transcendent mystical experience. The Godhead of the Perennial Philosophy is characterized as "pure, absolute, and eternal Reality" untainted by human-like traits. Meister Eckhart wrote:

The Godhead gave all things up to God. The Godhead is poor, naked and empty as though it were not; it has not, wills not, wants not, works not, gets not. It is God who has the treasure and the bride in him, the Godhead is as void as though it were not. God and Godhead are as distinct as heaven and earth, and even so the Godhead is above God. God becomes and disbecomes.

The distinction between God and Godhead is an obscure but important one, one that in the run-of-the-mill religious sermonizing is rarely mentioned, much less understood. But the distinction opens up an amazing possibility.

The Godhead, as you know, is characterized as simultaneously greater than infinity and less than zero. The Godhead is the ultimate and absolute source, the uncaused cause, the eternal intelligence that is literally no thing; the spaceless, timeless nothingness that is greater than all things. The Godhead is, for us, an unimaginable paradox.

So what then is God?

Turn for a moment to Kaballah. This is usually assumed to be an esoteric component of Judaism, yet according to the Kabbalist Rav Berg of the Kaballah Center:

*Kabbalah has nothing at all to do with religion. According to the ancient sages of Kaballah, God never imposed organized religion upon mankind. Religion is a man-made invention. Religion is a corruption of the power that the Light Force of God gave humanity 3,400 years ago on Mount Sinai. Kaballah is not a religion any more than quantum physics or Einstein's theory of relativity is a religion. (*Nano: Technology of Mind over Matter, *2008)*

In Kaballah the Godhead (also Brahman) is Ein-Sof. Kaballah scholar Gershom Sholem writes of Ein-Sof in his *Kaballah.*

The decision to emerge from concealment into manifestation and creation is not in any sense a process which is a necessary consequence of the essence of

Ein-Sof; it is a free decision which remains a constant and impenetrable mystery. God Who is called Ein-Sof in respect of Himself is called Ayin in respect of his first self-revelation.

WHAT DOES THIS MUMBO-JUMBO MEAN?

Imagine winning the jackpot in the state lottery. Suddenly there is a billion dollars in your bank account. Joy! Rapture!

But then comes the bad news. You are not allowed to withdraw or spend so much as a penny. It's yours to own, but there is not a thing you can do with it. What use is all the money in the world if it cannot be converted into useful products or desirable actions? I view the Godhead in this way. The Godhead has infinite potential, infinite power, infinite ability…but that is all sterile perfection.

In *The God Theory* the Godhead chooses to convert potential into experience. The "decision to emerge from concealment into manifestation and creation" is made by the Godhead. A part of the infinite nothingness becomes a reality. And it is that part of the infinite nothingness that is God the Creator. That is why Meister Eckhart wrote that "the Godhead is above God. God becomes and disbecomes."

The Godhead reveals a part of itself and that instance of the Godhead is God the Creator. The Godhead "dreams" into existence a kind of limited but still infinite—It is a mystery!—personification, or perhaps I should coin the term *deification* of itself. This is God the Creator whose role it is to bring into existence, via his consciousness, a universe.

And this I think is the origin of the Big Bang: the "emergence into manifestation and creation" of Ein-Sof. The resulting Universe is a finely tuned one in respect to its life-friendly laws of nature for the simple reason that that was its purpose.

I thus propose the following:

- The laws of nature of our Universe are the manifestation, the making real, of a few thoughts of the eternal intelligence, the pre-existing consciousness that is the Godhead. Its thoughts become the laws of nature and that is why the laws peculiar to our Universe are life-friendly.

- God the Creator is the part of the Godhead that comes to life in the creation dream of the Godhead to shepherd this creation into existence. That is why in the words of Meister Eckhart "God becomes." This also implies that if our Universe comes to an end, God the Creator "disbecomes" as the dream ends, but of course the Godhead continues. To be clear, God is not any kind of separate being from the Godhead, but merely a dynamic aspect of the Godhead. Think of the difference between who you truly are and the role you play on the job as a teacher, a businessman, an accountant...or even a scientist. A time may come to stop being the teacher or the businessman, but you cannot stop being yourself.

- The creation event could involve the coming into existence of both physical and non-physical realms, and in fact Kaballah explicitly claims that such other "worlds" exist. Science today recognizes only a physical realm, of course. On the other hand string theory demands the existence of additional dimensions which might house different universes.

- The physical creation event is none other than the Big Bang. The Big Bang is the physical creation event viewed from the inside.
- Everything in our Universe being a product of consciousness is therefore ultimately nothing but consciousness.

A MENTAL UNIVERSE

The notion that reality is purely physical can be traced back to the two 5th-century BC. Greek philosophers, Leucippus and his student Democritus. They are the founders of the concept of atoms as eternal indestructible things, and indeed the only things that truly exist. They are thus the first true reductionist materialists. Plato, on the other hand, proposed that our reality was merely a shadow world of a greater reality of ideas or forms. Precisely what is meant by *form* can be debated, but the key concept is that the physical realm is not the only one, and indeed is the lesser realm and owes its very existence to another ideal realm. It is interesting that one of the key founders of quantum mechanics, Werner Heisenberg, wrote of these two opposite perspectives on the ultimate nature of reality:

…it seems that, in spite of the tremendous success that the concept of the atom has achieved in modern science, Plato was very much nearer the truth about the structure of matter than Leucippus or Democritus. ("The Debate Between Plato and Democritus," in Quantum Questions, *K. Wilber, ed., 1984)*

In an essay published in *Nature* in 2005, Johns Hopkins professor Richard Conn Henry argues as well that the Universe must be ultimately immaterial in nature if quantum mechanics is taken seriously. Like Jeans he sees the Universe as entirely mental, and, citing Eddington:

It is difficult for the matter-of-fact physicist to accept the view that the substratum of everything is of a mental character.

Based on his interpretation of quantum mechanics he concludes his essay with the statement: "The Universe is immaterial—mental and spiritual." This is quite an amazing position for an essay published in *Nature* to take, but in fact, apart from terminology that a physicist might find somewhat unpalatable owing to philosophical biases, there is nothing whatsoever in any of these concepts about God that conflicts with the discoveries of science. Our scientific knowledge begins with the Big Bang.

Somewhere in the realm between theory and speculation lies the notion that string theory or inflation fields hold the key to the origin of our Universe. If there are many other universes then it is easy to explain away why ours appears to be special. (We could not exist under different conditions, so naturally we find ourselves here.) But that still does not explain how some whole ensemble of other universes came about. Are the string or inflation fields to be taken as pre-existing conditions? Uncaused causes?

Somewhere in the realm between mystical knowledge and speculation lies the notion that an infinite intelligence thought our Universe into existence. I prefer this explanation to the random universes explanation with its own unresolved causation problems, but either one is defensible. I propose

that the infinite intelligence explanation offers an amazing consequence: *that there is purpose for the Universe, that
this purpose is the conversion of potential into experience, and
that a key element in this scheme is the evolution of life-forms.*

This is where God needs help from Darwin.

THE QUESTION OF WHY

The Perennial Philosophy offers a profound spiritual interpretation based upon the acquisition of intuitive knowledge throughout history. It is very specific that our own essence is identical with that of God, and that the Universe is
the result of, hence ultimately reducible to, consciousness.
The one point on which, so far as I know, it is unclear is
"why?" Why would such a creation take place? What is the
purpose behind it?

Virtually all religions see human beings and other living things as separate from God. As to why God would do
such a thing as create a Universe in which life-forms separate from God would arise, the explanation frequently goes
along the lines of God wanting to have beings to love. This
is touted as a wonderful sign of a benevolent deity out to
love us...or at least those of us who toe the line and don't
irritate him or worse.

I think the explanation is simpler: God's consciousness
wishes to know itself by expressing itself. God wishes to
make his potential real. We already know from the Perennial Philosophy that our essence is the same as God's. The
implication is that we are, literally, each of us instances of
God experiencing his potential. God does not wish to be
our heavenly buddy, he *is* us and we are him. But obviously
we are God in a very limited way. The 12th-century French
abbot St. Bernard of Clairvaux wrote:

> *The spiritual creature which we are has need of a body, without which it could nowise attain that knowledge which it obtains as the only approach to those things, by knowledge of which it is made blessed.*

The spiritual creature having need of a body is God. The spiritual creature living in a body is us. God experiences his potential through us and through every other creature in the Universe, including, of course, animals such as my lovable but not very exciting pet turtle, Pogo. God's consciousness resides in and thus experiences every creature, and that is because Brahman and Atman are of the same essence. Kaballah scholar Daniel Matt writes:

> *By evolving through spacetime, by organizing Itself into the complex variety of existence, God grows and learns endlessly, discovering awareness through each of us— God's countless, inimitable selves…. In our cosmic game of hide-and-seek, God hides within each of us within all of creation and throughout spacetime…. God is disguised as the world, and the purpose of the game of creation is to uncover the divine, to explore the limits of who we are, to actualize God's self-awareness. Our very consciousness is the universe becoming aware of itself, God becoming aware of Itself…. Without us, God is incomplete. The divine sparks remain hidden, the divine potential is unrealized. (*God and the Big Bang*)

IF WE ARE GOD, WHY DON'T WE KNOW THAT?

Andrew Cohen and Ken Wilber are two influential contemporary spiritual thinkers. A recent dialogue took place between the two in the magazine *What is Enlightenment* on the purpose of the Universe, the importance of evolution, and the age-old question: what is it that we truly are?

Cohen: Before the Universe was born, there was only One, and that One had not yet become the Many... Why did the One become the Many?

That is the great mystery. If the One, the Godhead, is an absolutely perfect Spirit, resting in formless emptiness, delighting in its own eternal bliss and omniscience, not bound by space and time, why did it choose to "do something"? The One decided to create a Universe in which it could experience the Many. But the Many could not just be ready-made. To make what Wilber calls the "Kosmic game" interesting, novel, and adventurous, the many guises of the One would have to freely arise through the natural laws of the created Universe...including evolution. To make that work, though, the Many—that is, us—have to forget how the game started.

Wilber: ...you can't go through the whole process of evolution knowing you are God. That's just not going to work. So you would have to forget who you are; you'd have to get lost—convincingly get lost—or it's not a game and it's no fun at all! So you get lost and then you slowly awaken.... And then at some point evolution is going to become self-conscious, and then it's going to become superconscious. But it's taken fourteen billion years to get to this point.

In a sense the One is playing an elaborate game of hide-and-seek with itself. That is why our spiritual amnesia is so essential.

Wilber: There's only one way you can actually have a game with yourself.... You play the other person, and you forget that you are the other person. That amnesia, that ignorance, that avidya, is the primary ingredient of playing the game. So the Kosmic game, on the one hand, is a spontaneous lila or sport or play, a desire to throw yourself into myriad forms. And right next to that, co-emerging with it, is this ignorance, this forgetting. That's why Plato would say that all knowledge is just remembering.

Cohen: You realize I am the creator in the midst of the fact that there are six or seven billion other creators. But the ultimate truth is that I'm really the only one.... It becomes apparent that you have only two choices: you can either continue to do what you have been doing [which is nothing] forever, or you could do the only possible thing that you could do, which would be to endeavor to create a material universe in your own image.

ROLE OF EVOLUTION

Acting out a role on stage and living a real life are two very different things. I doubt any actor in his or her sane mind would wish to spend every waking moment acting out a script on stage instead of living a real life.

There is a direct analogy. The evolution of life-forms on Earth is a fact of science. Not only do I see no need for God to directly create or to microengineer the characteristics of life-forms, but I would also see such behavior as antithetical to the desire of God to experience himself. I propose that it is essential to the purpose of the Universe that once the set of laws has been determined and the Big Bang is off and running, letting the process of natural selection begin is the only way to initiate novelty. It is the new and unexpected that makes life interesting. God seeks novelty.

A compelling case that Darwin's theory provides insight into an intelligence that pours its creative essence into the universe and allows it free rein to go and make things happen is presented in *God After Darwin* by theologian John Haught. Instead of acting as a puppeteer who pulls strings, this God voluntarily relinquishes control to its creatures so that innovative possibilities may arise. Creation becomes more spicy with unplanned, unscripted, random possibilities that flow naturally as the result of this freedom. In creating the Universe, Haught suggests, God deliberately relinquishes omnipotence over this realm so as not to interfere with the free will of creation's beings. The Universe now has the opportunity to participate in its own crafting because of this ultimate expression of God's love.

Haught writes:

Love by its very nature can not compel, and so any God whose very essence is love should not be expected to overwhelm the world either with a coercively directive power or an annihilating presence. Indeed, an infinite love must in some ways absent or restrain itself, precisely in order to give the world the space in which to become something distinct from the creative love that constitutes it as other. We should anticipate, therefore, that any universe rooted in an unbounded love would have some features that appear to us as random and undirected.

An infinite intelligence able to experience its own potential is consistent with Darwin's ideas on random mutation and natural selection. In fact, Darwinian evolution via random mutation and natural selection allows God the opportunity to experience the outcome of his own potential through the adventures of incarnating and living in a diversity of life-forms.

"It would be contrary to the nature of providence and to the perfection of the world if nothing happened by chance," said Thomas Aquinas.

The experience-seeking purpose behind *The God Theory* includes a universe that teems with a continuum of life-forms and sentient beings, ranging from plants to animals to humans to presumably even more evolved beings elsewhere in the Universe. Darwinian science, contrary to the claims of reductionists, is not limited to a scientific ideology that is devoid of a God and that lacks any purpose. Darwin and God are really quite compatible, particularly when the goal is to actualize potential.

DOES CONSCIOUSNESS EVOLVE TO AN OMEGA POINT?

Teilhard de Chardin, the Jesuit paleontologist, proposed that evolution proceeds in a directional, goal-driven manner. "Omega Point" is the term he used to describe how consciousness evolves in an evolutionary process, and eventually converges toward a final unity. Teilhard's solution suggests a teleological view of evolution, but that is quite different from intelligent design. The capabilities of evolution are not denied; just reinterpreted by its driving force. Evolution proceeds by coaxing life-forms toward future perfection, not just through random mutation, suggests Teilhard.

Although a coaxing towards future perfection may not be detectable by conventional scientific measurements, I suggest that the evolution of living things occurs through a combination of physical and deterministic processes together with a higher-order principle which we have only begun to glimpse. There appears to be a self-creative, self-organizing character to living things that suggests the influence of a higher order. In addition, "wiggle room" allows chance and contingency to yield an innovative range of outcomes in the evolutionary process. Reductionists assume instead that, for living things, order and information somehow emerge solely from elementary physical processes, because they believe that only mindless matter is real.

It is interesting that physicist Wolfgang Pauli expressed skepticism about the ability of nothing more than random mutation driving evolution to ever greater complexity. Werner Heisenberg summarized Pauli's view as follows.

...Pauli is also skeptical of the Darwinian opinion, extremely widespread in modern biology, whereby the evolution of species on Earth is supposed to have come about solely according to the laws of physics and chemistry, through chance mutations and their subsequent effects. He feels this scheme too narrow and considers the possibility of more general connections, which can neither be fitted into the general conceptual scheme of causal structures nor be properly described by the term "chance." (In Quantum Questions, K. Wilber, ed., 1984)

Admittedly I am more drawn by the philosophical appeal of Teilhard's Omega Point than persuaded by his presentation of a believable mechanism, something he was unable to produce. Teilhard presents a tantalizing implication of an evolutionary hope that is developed on a cosmic scale. He claims that the universe will evolve towards ultimate perfection, rather than descend into a final state of maximum entropy.

This particular creation (of which there may be an infinite number) will someday be complete, he claims, as the result of the laws of natural selection in the physical realm and, in my view, the workings of karma in the spiritual realm. It will become all that it can be ultimately, and it will fulfill its potential and thereby enrich God. Being transformed by living in and experiencing the Universe, every experience of each consciousness will return to the infinite intelligence from which it was born. I favor Teilhard's spiritual hope rather than the pessimistic view of an ultimate state of a universe composed of maximum entropy.

When mystics say that the Universe is the body of God, they endlessly annoy reductionists, whose reaction is to shrug off the statement as either poetic or just plain crazy. Very few reductionists try to understand the mystics' true meaning. Their "body of God" is more than just poetic metaphor, claim philosophers such as Huxley and Teilhard. It is maintained that there is truth embedded in the mystics' claim, one that we can at least tentatively understand, if not fully comprehend in the Perennial Philosophy, the Omega Point, and *The God Theory* itself. This truth, that God lives through us, is the foundation on which we can build a humane and optimistic spiritual worldview.

7

STAYING OUT OF HEAVEN

Eternity is a very long time, especially towards the end.

—Woody Allen

One of the scariest thoughts I have ever had was about being in heaven. Here's the problem: it never stops. The one characteristic of heaven that seems to be held across the board in religions is that your stay in heaven will last forever. The promise is one of everlasting happiness. But that is an oxymoron. Anything you do, no matter how pleasurable at first, can become tedious and eventually

135

even unbearable. And in an infinite amount of time anything whatsoever is guaranteed to become an ordeal. The very idea of something going on and on and on, with no end ever possible is, to me, the ultimate nightmare.

This point was made in a 1960 episode of the wonderfully creative television program *The Twilight Zone*. The program begins, as usual, with a cigarette-smoking Rod Serling, the host and mastermind of the series, declaiming:

> *Portrait of a man at work, the only work he's ever done, the only work he knows. His name is Henry Francis Valentine, but he calls himself "Rocky," because that's the way his life has been—rocky and perilous and up-hill at a dead run all the way. He's tired now, tired of running or wanting, of waiting for the breaks that come to others but never to him, never to Rocky Valentine. A scared, angry little man. He thinks it's all over now, but he's wrong. For Rocky Valentine, it's just the beginning.* (Reprinted with the permission of Don Congdon Associates, Inc.)

The story opens with Rocky robbing a pawnshop. He shoots a night watchman and a policeman before he himself is killed by another policeman. He wakes up, apparently unharmed, somewhere in the company of a pleasant character named Pip who claims to be Rocky's guide and who says he is under instructions to grant Rocky's every wish. Naturally Rocky assumes that he has—miraculously—gone to heaven and here is what must be his guardian angel. How wonderful. Life goes on in a seemingly endless granting of wishes and good fortune. He plays games and, of course, always comes out the winner. He seeks attention from beautiful women and is never rebuffed. This goes on and on to the point where Rocky is thoroughly satiated, bored, and has had enough of heaven. In desperation he begs Pip to send him to "the other place."

A diabolically bemused Pip replies: "This *is* the other place."

The show ends with Rod Serling's closing commentary.

"A scared, angry little man who never got a break. Now he has everything he's ever wanted—and he's going to have to live with it for eternity...in the Twilight Zone."

Really try to imagine the endless repetition and what it would feel like to know that something is never ever going to stop. If the thought does not frighten you, you probably have not let the full weight of forever sink in. It gives me the chills.

My own philosophical opinion is that it is not logically possible for time to go on forever, although of course I am open to astrophysical observations regarding the expansion of the Universe. The God of the Perennial Philosophy does not live forever in time. In the view of the Perennial Philosophy, God is external to the time stream, not bound by space and time. Such a thing is impossible for us to picture. If God is outside of time, does that not render him as inert and lifeless as a museum tableau? Indeed, the Godhead is described as being devoid of activity, unchangeable, absolute and perfect.

As Taoist sage Lao Tzu put it: It is serene. Empty. Solitary. Unchanging. Infinite. Eternally present.

It must remain the deepest of mysteries how such a static state can be one of absolute perfection and greater than we can imagine, and yet not exist in time.

It is sometimes joked that time is what keeps everything from happening all at once. There is more than a little truth in that. The spacetime environment allows God's consciousness to fragment into countless individual consciousnesses experiencing separation and interaction with each other, such as you and me. Perhaps time thus becomes a tool for God to evolve his own essence. But that is just a guess.

Another thing that is very problematic about heaven is the entry requirements. The kinds of circumstances people are born into and the situations we face in life are tremendously varied. And yet we are supposedly fairly judged as ready for heavenly prime time or not based on one run through of life. An infant who manages to just make it to baptism before choking on her pacifier would appear to have the ultimate free ticket...do not pass go, go directly to heaven. There is something deeply arbitrary and troubling about this arrangement.

The heaven concept also raises the dilemma about what to do with the rotten apples of the world. Would a deathbed change-of-heart be enough to let a Hitler or Stalin through the Pearly Gates? Most everyone would say no, so clearly if you are going to have a classical heaven and a one-chance-to-make-it rule, you've got to create a hell for the really bad characters...which of course most religions claim.

THE STANDARD MODEL OF LIFE

Recall that Atman and Brahman are identical in essence. That being the case, God would have to be sending part of himself to hell in what, in an analogy to physics, might be called the "standard model" of life as espoused by Western religions defined as:

- Being created by, but separate from God.
- Incarnating only once.
- Being rewarded or punished for that one lifetime by entry into an everlasting heaven or hell.

I propose an alternative God Theory model of life.

- Being a spark of God's consciousness that thinks it is separate from God.
- Incarnating numerous times.
- Having as many life opportunities as necessary to achieve a state that can reunite with God.

Several obvious problems inherent in the standard model are easily disposed of in *The God Theory* model. First of all, it levels the playing field with respect to life circumstances. The rapacious tycoon out to get his billions at the expense of others might well have to live a few future lives as a bum on the street to balance his bad behavior and advance his way to enlightenment.

It also solves the hell problem. Clearly a Hitler or Stalin have a lot of attitude adjustment and karmic compensation ahead of them. But it seems to me to make more sense that this takes place via however many future lives are necessary under appropriate circumstances, rather than creating a hell for the scoundrels.

As for heaven, if we are all sparks of God then there is no need for a celestial paradise where beings who are separate from God—us—can hobnob with cherubim and seraphim forever after in purported perpetual happiness. Heaven is instead a complete awakening from the delusion of separation from God and thus reunion with God.

And finally, it does away with the creation-out-of-nothing problem: the belief that something such as our Universe is simply conjured up. This may not bother most people on the grounds that of course God should be able to make something out of nothing. That is what religions widely tout as God power. But it seems somewhat more logical that God should be all there is, that there can be nothing that is truly separate. So God does not have to snap divine fingers and pull rabbits and universes out of hats. Instead all of creation is just a part of God, a part that has been "fenced off," so to speak to let the rules of the Universe take their course, letting life originate and evolve so that some of God's consciousness can enter into those life-forms and thus experience some of God's potential.

My view is that creation of something out of nothing is impossible and that God is all there is. God can create apparent realities—such as our Universe—but this "creation" is still part of God. God can, so to speak, "fence off" a part of him/herself to appear to be a separate and independent reality, but ultimately that is an illusion, something like a dream of God. We are living such a dream, but we are really just a part of God doing so, even though our seeming independence and separateness appear quite real. The point of creating realities is to bring about experience of the possibilities afforded by that reality, hence God's potential becomes God's experience.

If God could create something out of nothing, where would that ability stop? Why could God not create another God, which in turn could create another God, and pretty soon you could have an infinite number of Gods. Where would they all find gainful Godly level employment? Too many unemployed Gods could put a strain on the system. I'm being partially facetious, but think about it.

CREATION BY SUBTRACTION

To try to picture this view of creation, think of how you can use a prism to get blue or red out of a beam of white light. A rainbow works this way. The little droplets of water in the air refract the white light of the Sun, and what emerges is a rainbow of colors, all of which were part of the white light before they were separated out. The colors did not come out of nothing. They came out of everything, rhetorically speaking: the totality of the white light. Who would have guessed that white light was a composite of all the colors, that they were all hidden? Well, actually the answer is Isaac Newton.

Think of how a slide or film projector works. A bright white light is shone through a filter—the film or the slide—which absorbs the white light in just the right way to create an image. Here everything but blue is filtered; there everything but red, etc. The net result of the leftover filtered light that emerges is an image. It results from selective subtraction of the white light. The white light is the potential source of an infinite variety of images. Any image can be created by just the right spatial filtering of the white light. The image is created by subtraction from the white light.

I propose that in a roughly analogous fashion, God subtracts all but some of his infinite potential in some, for lack of better words, spiritual space. The remainder in that spiritual space, which Kabbalists characterize as the void, becomes the creation. In our case this is the physical universe and it begins with literally a Big Bang. Our Universe hence did not come out of nothing. It came out of everything, which is God. It is a tiny bit of the infinite source that is God, a tiny bit with just the right remaining ingredients to make a rich, viable, life-generating Universe.

GOD AS TIMELESS ABSOLUTE

The Perennial Philosophy asserts that God, the ground of all being, is ultimately a "no thing," an Absolute being beyond all attributes, "pure, absolute, and eternal reality." St. John of the Cross writes:

(The saints in heaven) who know him most perfectly per-ceive most clearly that He is infinitely incomprehensible.

The "Clear Light of the Void" of Mahayana Buddhism is, according to Huxley, the same as the sinking into noth-ingness that Meister Eckhart urges:

Thou must love God as not-God, not-Spirit, not-person, not-image, but as He is, a sheer, pure absolute One, sundered from all two-ness, and in whom we must eternally sink from nothingness to nothingness.

True knowledge of this God can only happen by union with him in the mystical experience, not by rational analysis or intellectual reasoning. That direct knowledge transcends intellectual knowledge.

That said, this is a book. It cannot do anything but try to be rational and analytical. It cannot bestow the experience of union with the Absolute on the reader. That's beyond the power of the printed word. There is no choice but to ap-proach the concept of God with words.

If God is described as a being of perfect love and un-ending bliss, that strikes us as a good thing. After all, love and bliss are things we seek ourselves, that make us happy. There is, of course, the complication that a "being" that is "no thing" is hard to *grok*, i.e. understand in the colorful parlance of the late science fiction writer Robert Heinlein. But owing to the attractiveness of love and bliss, we can probably tolerate some uneasiness over the "no thing" as-pect of God while identifying with the love and bliss aspects.

God as the Absolute is also described as existing in a realm beyond space and time in a state of perfect, unchanging, unmoving, never-ending repose. This is much more difficult to grok. Perhaps to some it even seems scary. It makes me cringe a bit. Is God a frozen still-life? Is God as inert as a dead man? This does not sound at all attractive. And if true, how could such a God create a Universe when the act of creation must involve action and change?

As an astrophysicist I am quite familiar with the spacetime concept in Einstein's relativity. There is no way to accommodate a no-space, no-time existence capable of creation in spacetime as I know it. I can only conclude that our physical existence is so wrapped up in space and time that we cannot rationally even imagine how something could exist and even be dynamic without operating in space and time. From within our spacetime vantage point, a timeless, unchanging God who creates universes is as incomprehensible as the proverbial square circle. And yet timelessness is part of the mystical experience...along with a loss of self (ego), merger with a greater unity, intensified meaning, and a sense of the transcendent and sacred.

The mystical experience sometimes includes perceiving thousands, or even millions of years of history of the Earth in a real time that lasts only minutes.

Physicist Lee Smolin has written about time:

I have been studying the question of what time is for much of my adult life. But I must admit...that I am no closer to an answer now than I was then. Indeed, even after all this study, I do not think we can answer even the simple question: 'What sort of thing is time?' (How Things Are, 1995)

And from a much older era we hear St. Augustine.

What then is time? If no one asks me, I know; if I want to explain it to a questioner, I do not know.

The traditional view of God is that he is outside of time, that he sees all things in an eternal present, as Thomas Aquinas states:

*[God's] knowledge, like his existence, is measured by eternity, which in one and the same instant encompasses all time; so his gaze is eternally focused on everything in time as on something present.... What happens in time is known by us in time, moment by moment, but by God in an eternal moment, above time. (*Summa Theologiæ *14.13)*

EXPERIENCING TIMELESSNESS

An experience of timelessness is a key part of the cosmic consciousness event had by Dr. Allan Smith. At the time, Smith, an MD, was 38 years old. He was a Board Certified anesthesiologist, a faculty member of the University of California San Francisco, and a recent winner of the American Heart Association's Wright prize.

His experience began spontaneously while he was alone and sitting in an easy chair watching an exceptionally beautiful sunset through a floor-to-ceiling window. He began to notice an increase in light seemingly from all directions and not at all associated with the setting sun. The light gave the impression of thickening the air itself. He then reports:

Along with the light came an alteration in mood. I began to feel very good, then still better, then elated. While this was happening, the passage of time seemed to become slower and slower. The brightness, mood-elevation, and time-slowing all progressed together. It is difficult to estimate the time period over which these changes occurred, since the sense of time was itself affected. However, there was a feeling of continuous change, rather than a discrete jump or jumps to a new state. Eventually, the sense of time passing stopped entirely. It is difficult to describe this feeling, but perhaps it would be better to say that there was no time, or no sense of time. Only the present moment existed. My elation proceeded to an ecstatic state, the intensity of which I had never even imagined could be possible. The white light around me merged with the reddish light of the sunset to become one all enveloping, intense undifferentiated light field. Perception of other things faded. Again, the changes seemed to be continuous. At this point, I merged with the light, and everything, including myself, became one unified whole. There was no separation between myself and the rest of the universe. (*Smith and Tart,* Journal of Consciousness Studies, *1998*)

He then goes on to say how words fail, or simply do not exist, to adequately even begin to describe the experience. How do you experience anything when time is at a standstill? We do not have words that can convey this. In fact, we cannot even imagine it. Experience without time is simply impossible to imagine in our everyday state. But, words or not, the experience is utterly real. Smith talks about the absolute "knowingness," a "deep understanding that occurs without words." As others have also written, the knowledge that comes with the experience is more real than any ordinary everyday knowledge.

Smith found himself united with God. Not the rewarding, punishing, demanding, sometimes wrathful God of many religions, but rather a God that is the Universe itself. He writes:

The universe could no more be separate from God than my body could be separate from its cells. Moreover, the only emotion that I would associate with God is love, but it would be more accurate to say that God is love than God is loving.

Mystical vs. Psychedelic

As interesting and significant as this experience was, a follow up set of experiments took place, which were unique. About a month after the cosmic consciousness experience Smith took the first of several LSD trips. He did this partially to see if he could recapture the experience, and partially as a researcher to directly compare the two types of states. This eventually led to a collaboration with Charles Tart, a professor at the University of California at Davis and an internationally recognized researcher in consciousness and especially altered states of consciousness.

Many people have reported the kind of mystical experience that Smith had. Others have written about the sometimes profound, mystical-like aspects of psychedelics. And although some have tried to compare the two, never had this been done and published by someone who actually had both types of experience. It is one thing to compare verbal descriptions, or a verbal description of one state with the experience of the other. But it is a unique thing to compare the actual inner experiences. In 1998 Smith and Tart published "Cosmic Consciousness Experience and Psychedelic Experiences: A First Person Comparison" in the *Journal of Consciousness Studies*.

On direct comparison they proved to be very different states of consciousness.

During the LSD trip time slowed down, but unlike the cosmic consciousness experience, it did not stop. The psychedelic mood was "brittle," meaning it could shift: wax or wane and alternate between pleasant and unpleasant, ecstatic and frightening. The cosmic consciousness experience evolved consistently and was uniformly pleasant and all-pervasive. In fact, more than pleasant. On an admittedly imprecise scale the mood of cosmic consciousness was 10 times better than the "best orgasm."

But the two biggest differences were that, first, the ego, the self, receded in the LSD experience but never entirely disappeared as it did when Smith united with God in his cosmic consciousness experience. And second, the knowing insight into the meaning and significance of the other reality faded away after the drug trip. It was illusory. On the other hand, the cosmic consciousness insight on the nature of a greater reality was so certain that Smith writes:

> *I could more easily be convinced that the computer at which I now sit is illusory than I could be convinced that CC (cosmic consciousness) was.*

He wrote that more than 20 years after the experience.

CAN YOU REALLY TRAIN FOR ENLIGHTENMENT?

The experience of John Wren-Lewis, a mathematical physicist, had a different cause. He had a near-death experience from being poisoned on a bus by a would-be thief. Prior to the event he regarded himself as a "Freud-style skeptic about all things mystical," someone who "saw mysticism as a neurotic escape into fantasy and despised spiritual seekers." But in 1983 in a hospital bed in Thailand he had what he calls "God consciousness" thrust upon him.

Upon awakening he found himself as if being reborn, re-created in fact, from out of a "vast blackness that was somehow radiant, a kind of infinite concentrated aliveness of 'pure consciousness' that has no separation within it, and therefore no space or time."

He felt himself emerging from a state of eternity, and that the pure consciousness of that state "loves all the productions of time." This "eternity consciousness" continued to persist years afterwards. He goes on to say:

> *The main point I want to make here, however, is that perhaps the most extraordinary feature of eternity consciousness is that it doesn't feel extraordinary at all. It feels quintessentially natural that personal consciousness should be aware of its own Ground, while my first*

fifty-nine years of so-called "normal" consciousness, in ignorance of that Ground, now seem like a kind of waking dream. It was as if I'd been entranced from birth into a collective nightmare of separate individuals struggling in an alien universe for survival, satisfaction and significance.

My intensive investigations in this area over the past decade have left me in no doubt that proponents of the so-called Perennial Philosophy are correct in identifying a common "deep structure" of experience underlying the widely different cultural expressions of mystics in all traditions. Nonetheless I find no evidence whatever for the often-made claim that these traditions contain disciplines for attaining God consciousness that have been empirically tested and verified. (What Is Enlightenment? *Vol. 4, 1995*)

He comes to a conclusion that contradicts conventional spiritual seeker wisdom: that the perfecting of character and mindset over years and years can lead to a state of enlightenment. Indeed, he concludes that "the very idea of a spiritual path is necessarily self-defeating, because it does the one thing that has to be undone if there is to be awakening to eternity: it concentrates attention firmly on 'futurity.'" To Wren-Lewis the enlightened state is always attainable here and now if only we could wake up. It is the preoccupation with time—even time spent seeking enlightenment—that "drives eternity out of awareness." In this context, the "I want it now" attitude—anathema to seekers—may actually be the correct one. The waking up is, of course, the difficult part.

A WORLD OF POLARITY

A major mystery of the Absolute God is why he would create anything when he is already perfect. I have theorized in *The God Theory* that by creating universes in which life-forms can arise and evolve, God is able to experience his potential, and that he seeks this experience. But why would an already perfect being do this?

If, as the mystical experiences indicate, God is perfect, why do we live in such a seemingly imperfect world?

First of all, the mystical experiences claim that when somehow consciousness expands to include the entire universe, all is perfection. To those of us living in the flawed and violent realm of 21st-century Earth, this is almost insulting. What kind of Polyannish, eyes-closed, wishful thinking is going on here? Who can deny the horrible things that happen here every single day?

My intuition is that the mystical sense of perfection stems from the grokking of the universe in its totality of space and in the fullness of time. Like a building under construction, what looks like a mess now may be a work of utter beauty when completed.

But why is there imperfection to begin with? A physical universe as a place for experiences and the experiences themselves require the interplay of opposites, of polarity. You cannot experience light without darkness. Heat is only heat in comparison to cold. The world of experience requires opposites for its very existence. You could not feel or see or sense anything without the contrast of an opposite. There is no more vision in a world of only pure white light than there is in a world of complete darkness.   .

The realm of the Absolute cannot support experience. It takes a universe of contrast and polarity. In order to experience, the Absolute God must somehow create a realm in which imperfection has a role to play. That is seemingly what he did in triggering the Big Bang.

8

CONSCIOUSNESS AND REALITY

To say that consciousness creates the world of matter is a nice florid philosophical statement. But is there any hard evidence that this could be the case? Experiments carried out in 2007 by one of the world's foremost quantum optics groups, published in *Nature,* support this idea. As reported in the British science magazine, *New Scientist*:

> *Recent experiments led by a group at the University of Vienna, Austria, provide the most compelling evidence yet that there is no objective*

151

reality beyond what we observe…. The researchers take this to mean we have to abandon the idea of an objective reality.

The story behind this begins with the Heisenberg uncertainty principle, formulated in 1927, one of the central elements of quantum physics and the key ingredient in the experiment. It highlights one of the most important differences between classical (Newtonian) physics and quantum physics. In classical physics the position and velocity of an object can *in principle* be determined to an infinitely accurate precision. (This was the origin of the deterministic nightmare supposedly precluding human free will discussed in Chapter 4.) The Heisenberg uncertainty principle rules out infinite precision in both position and velocity, not because of any sloppiness in measurement, but because of an intrinsic fuzziness in nature itself (see the discussion of the wave function in Chapter 2).

The Heisenberg uncertainty principle is illustrated in Figure 6 on the next page. The tall curve on the left in row 1 depicts a measurement of the velocity of something. The spread shows that the *velocity* is not precisely known, but on the other hand the velocity is more precisely known than the instantaneous *position* of the object shown on the right, which is spread even more. Now you can choose to measure the instantaneous position more accurately (row 2 and row 3), but the tradeoff is that the velocity measurement becomes correspondingly more spread out. This is a fundamental law of nature on the quantum level.

The next development is the attempt by Einstein in 1935 to disprove the Heisenberg uncertainty principle via what came to be called the Einstein-Podolsky-Rosen (EPR) thought experiment.

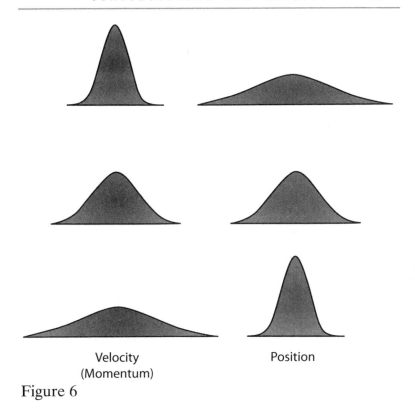

Velocity
(Momentum)   Position

Figure 6

A thought experiment is a purely mental exercise whose consequences can be thought through to provide insight or to suggest a real test. You make some assumption that you wish to test, and then imagine a situation in which this assumption would predict a certain outcome. If experience tells us whether that predicted outcome would result, or not, under those circumstances, that verifies or refutes the assumption. Of course, since it is a thought experiment rather than a real one, the experience-based outcome that serves as the test might be mistaken. Thought experiments made by a 19th-century pre-quantum physicist about measuring positions and velocities, for example, would turn out to lead to the wrong conclusion as shown by real subsequent quantum experiments. The world is sometimes different than imagined.

Einstein's EPR thought experiment suggested a way around the Heisenberg uncertainty principle, but in this case there was no way to actually verify or refute it with a measurement. A variation on EPR that was more feasible was formulated by David Bohm in 1951. The Bohm version of EPR was developed into a real testable experiment by John Bell in 1964. But it was not until 1982 that Bell's experiment was carried out, and when it was, it proved Einstein wrong and Heisenberg right.

Einstein being wrong! That in and of itself is of considerable interest. But the deepest implications were yet to come.

In 2003, Nobel Laureate Anthony Leggett published a more rigorous version of the Bell experiment. It took some time to devise a way to test the Leggett version, but Markus Aspelmeyer of the Austrian Academy of Sciences and Anton Zeilinger of the University of Vienna succeeded. This particular experimental verification of quantum laws, including the Heisenberg uncertainty principle, has the profoundest of consequences.

Their results, published in 2007, suggest

...that there is nothing inherently real about the properties of an object that we measure. In other words, measuring those properties is what brings them into existence.

Or as quantum researcher Vlatko Vedral of the University of Leeds puts it:

*Rather than passively observing it, we in fact create re-
ality. (*New Scientist, *June 23, 2007)*

We examine the history of this amazing conclusion.

THE HEISENBERG
UNCERTAINTY PRINCIPLE

The world of 100 years ago was a lot simpler, both tech-
nologically and conceptually. Evidence for the existence
of atoms as the building blocks of matter was beginning to
emerge from the laboratories of the day, but it was naturally
assumed that these new particles would follow the same laws
of physics that governed such recent inventions as steam engines, light bulbs, and telephones. At first it appeared that
atoms were like miniature solar systems, with lightweight
electrons orbiting heavy nuclei like planets whirling around
the Sun.

Unfortunately this idea would not work because electrons carry electric charge. It was already well known that
electric charge orbiting around a nucleus would emit radiation and thereby the electron would lose energy and quickly
spiral into the nucleus, in less than a billionth of a second
for that matter. A radically new view of nature was necessary at the level of the atom. The resolution of the stable
atom problem led to a revolution in physics: quantum
mechanics.

With the coming of quantum mechanics, atoms, and
many other particles that have been discovered since were
found to obey a wholly new and different set of laws from
those that reigned in the large-scale world of everyday human experience. In the ordinary world we assume that we

can, with the proper equipment, determine quite precisely the instantaneous position and speed of a car, a train, or a runner, for example. From the view of quantum mechanics, this ability to measure precisely is actually an illusion, although an almost correct one in the ordinary world. The fact of the matter is, though, that if we measure the speed of a race car at the moment that it crosses the finish line and if we know the position of the finish line to within the width of a human hair, the speed will be uncertain by a billionth billionth billionth millionth of a mile per hour.

How could this possibly matter? In fact, for the situation of a car, it doesn't matter in the slightest. But there are experiments with important philosophical implications for which such minute uncertainties matter a great deal.

Position and velocity (technically momentum, which is mass times velocity) for the same object are "incommensurable quantities" at the quantum level. That means you can't simultaneously measure both exactly.

This is a reflection of the Heisenberg uncertainty principle, formulated by German physicist Werner Heisenberg in 1927, while he was working at Niels Bohr's research institute in Copenhagen (and had some time on his hands when Bohr was gone on a skiing holiday). Now of course in real life, the inaccuracy that comes with any measuring device gives far less accuracy than this quantum effect. You could never notice such a small quantum effect as the race car in the everyday world.

But let's assume that instead of knowing the position of that race car at a given instant to the width of a human hair, we managed to know it with *absolute* precision. What would that do to the corresponding uncertainty in the measurable velocity? This is where such a quantum effect becomes really interesting, because the answer is that if the position were known with complete precision, the measured velocity could range anywhere between zero and the speed of light. Of course, knowing the position with perfect precision is perfectly impossible. But on the small scale of particles, one can imagine the Heisenberg uncertainty principle might yield some interesting effects...and it does.

SUPERSEDING THE CLOCKWORK UNIVERSE

There are two profound consequences of the Heisenberg uncertainty principle. First of all, the act of measuring introduces an inescapable uncertainty. No matter how small this effect might be, it destroys the "clockwork universe" as a picture of reality. For the role of consciousness in the Universe this is a terrifically good thing. The "clockwork universe" refers to the classical physics of Newton. It came with a disturbing metaphysical consequence: determinism, utter and complete determinism leading, in effect, to a completely preordained reality. By that is meant that if the position and velocity of every particle in the Universe were precisely known at any moment in time, the rest of the future could be predicted with inescapable certainty. Like the steady, reliable motion of a clock, the Universe would tick away.

Unfortunately we ourselves are included in that Universe. And if we think of ourselves as just complex organic machines, then every thought and every action that we think we are consciously and freely choosing is in reality just the consequence of the previous state of the Universe. There is no freedom, there is no true choice, not in the slightest. In this view, we ourselves are no more than wind-up dolls, automatons, executing the thoughts and actions that we inherited from everything that came before us. Every choice we make is illusory from this perspective, because even the atoms and molecules in our brain are just following the positions and motions they inherited. The universe becomes like a giant billiard table whose countless billiard balls (the particles making up matter) are just following the laws of mechanics: the 5-ball hits the 9-ball knocking the 8-ball in the pocket and that explains why I just scratched my head thinking I was doing so of my own free will.

In this view we were born with every thought we would ever have in our lives already preprogrammed, and so our thinking would be no more free and spontaneous than a CD playing from start to finish. One could, in principle, have predicted every note of Mozart's opera "The Marriage of Figaro" or Beethoven's Ninth Symphony by examining in minute atom-by-atom detail the configuration of the Earth on any given day when the dinosaurs were roaming.

This is a truly depressing view of our own nature. Fortunately, the Heisenberg uncertainty principle renders this dreary view impossible. You can never predict the future from the past because of this intrinsic uncertainty. Choice and free will are possible thanks to quantum physics.

Thank goodness!

The second consequence concerns what is real. The more precisely we measure x, the less we know about y. Now the question is, does this mean that y has some precise real value that the Heisenberg uncertainty principle obscures from sight? In other words, is y precise and real but partially hidden by the quirkiness of quantum laws? Or on the contrary, is it possible that y does not actually exist until it is brought into existence by the act of its measurement and thereby becomes real only up to whatever fuzzy reality the Heisenberg uncertainty principle allows?

Clearly, the Heisenberg uncertainty principle has profound implications. It provides the wiggle room for consciousness to use to exert itself and, as will unfold momentarily, leads even to the conclusion, based upon recent experiments, that "there is no objective reality beyond what we observe," suggesting that consciousness creates reality.

THE EINSTEIN-PODOLSKY-ROSEN (EPR) THOUGHT EXPERIMENT

In 1999, Albert Einstein was selected as the "Man of the Century" by *Time* magazine. He was also a spiritual thinker who famously wrote that "God does not play dice with the Universe." This was a dig at quantum laws and especially the Heisenberg uncertainty principle. But there is a giant paradox here. Einstein believed in the classical, deterministic reality embodied in Newtonian physics. His special and general theories of relativity modified Newtonian physics in a major way, but did not change the assumed underlying determinism. He was convinced that there must be determinism in quantum theory as well.

But because he believed in a God (of sorts), it is hard to imagine that he thought of humans as machine-like automatons acting in mindless response to the clockwork universe with its billiard-ball motion of particles determining all of reality, including our behavior. Without free will, humans, and other living things, would effectively be preprogrammed robots, their destiny immutably set—our destiny immutably set—by the precise configuration of every atom and molecule in our bodies, which traces back to the previous history of each such particle, in principle all the way back to the beginning of the Universe. It takes the Heisenberg uncertainty principle to provide the niche for free will. Thus it is quite an irony that Einstein's attempts to disprove quantum theory resulted, during the next 70 years, in the very experiments that would *validate* the Heisenberg uncertainty principle and lead to the evidence that consciousness creates reality.

In this context we might guess that Einstein would have been happy to be wrong.

But going back in time, Einstein was originally enthusiastic about quantum theory. Soon, though, he came to be a skeptic. In 1930, only three years after the formulation of the Heisenberg uncertainty principle, Einstein proposed a thought experiment at a Sixth Solvay Conference on Physics in Brussels. He was now convinced that it was possible to sneak around the Heisenberg uncertainty principle and thereby show that there is a precise reality in which, for example, positions and velocities of a given particle have definite values and that these definite values can be determined with total precision under the proper clever circumstances.

Note the word "determined." That is the key. Einstein was devising a clever way to determine such things as positions and velocities of particles precisely without having to directly measure them, and thereby create the quantum disturbance associated with measurement. If he could show that this was possible, it would demonstrate that quantum theory was not complete. If Einstein could precisely determine properties of quantum objects that quantum measurement would fail to measure precisely—owing to the Heisenberg uncertainty principle—then clearly quantum physics would be missing something.

In 1935, Einstein and two of his postdoctoral students, Boris Podolsky and Nathan Rosen, published a now famous paper that challenged the Heisenberg uncertainty principle: "Can Quantum Mechanical Description of Physical Reality Be Considered Complete?"

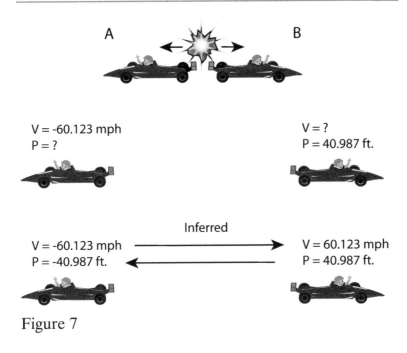

A   B

V = -60.123 mph   V = ?
P = ?   P = 40.987 ft.

Inferred

V = -60.123 mph   ——————————————————→   V = 60.123 mph
P = -40.987 ft.   ←——————————————————   P = 40.987 ft.

Figure 7

In a nutshell they argued as follows (as illustrated in Figure 7): Assume that two identical race cars, call them A and B, are initially at rest and that they are somehow then propelled—by a mini-explosion, say—In opposite directions with an exactly even and opposite force. At a given instant, we can measure the *velocity* (V) of car A with perfect precision even according to the Heisenberg uncertainty principle, knowing that we thereby sacrifice any possibility of simultaneously measuring its position since they are incommensurate quantities at the quantum level. Let's say we measure that velocity to be minus 60.123 mph where the minus simply means going to the left.

Similarly, we can measure the *position* (P) of car B with perfect precision at that instant even according to the Heisenberg uncertainty principle, knowing that we thereby sacrifice any possibility of simultaneously measuring its position at that instant. Call the position 40.987 feet.

But wait. Owing to conservation of momentum, if the precisely measured velocity of A is minus 60.123 mph at a given instant in time, then the precise velocity of B must be positive 60.123 mph at that same time. Similarly, if the precisely measured position of B is 40.987 feet, then the precise position of A must be minus 40.987 feet. We have apparently succeeded in determining the precise position of A and the precise velocity of B without having had to measure these quantities directly, thereby running afoul of Heisenberg. They can be inferred with perfect precision from the value of the other car thanks to the conservation of momentum law.

Einstein believed that this thought experiment demonstrated that there were indeed precise values of position and velocity for each particle that could be determined in this indirect way. He felt certain that both determinism and an objective reality could be coaxed even from quantum theory via his clever trick.

Einstein was wrong…but it would take years to prove that.

BOHM

David Bohm was a brilliant physicist. During World War II he was asked by Robert Oppenheimer to come to Los Alamos to work on the top secret atomic bomb Manhattan Project before even completing his PhD thesis. Unfortunately his youthful involvement with "radical politics" led to his being denied a security clearance. This led to a Catch-22 situation. Bohm remained at the University of California in Berkeley doing work that proved to be useful to the Manhattan Project, but when his thesis work was classified prior to completion, he was forbidden to write up his own thesis. He could not access his own work. Even the government could not stop him from thinking about his own work, but he could no longer write it down!

Soon after the war, in 1951, Bohm, by then an untenured professor at Princeton University—and about to be hounded out of the country for refusing to testify in the House Un-American Activities Committee—wrote a textbook in which he took a close look at EPR. The EPR paradox had remained a lingering philosophical thorn in the side of quantum theory for 16 years. Bohm hit upon a variation in the experiment that might make it more feasible. He realized that spin afforded a better version of the EPR test.

One of the built-in properties of fundamental particles, such as an electron or even that particle of light called the photon, is that they spin like a top. It would be more accurate to say that they have the property of spin, because for reasons that will become clear they cannot literally be rotating. Most physicists would argue that the spin is more of an "as if" characteristic. But for the following there is no harm in imagining a real spinning motion.

The convention for measuring spin is literally in your hands. Gently curl the fingers of your right hand and raise your thumb. Your fingers show the direction of the spinning motion and your thumb, pointing perpendicular to your fingers, shows the axis of the spin.

Define three directions at right angles to each other: up, north, and east. The axis of a gyroscope can point in any of these directions, and it is easy to measure the component in each of the directions. For example, the spin may lie mainly in the up-direction, say, and be partially tilted toward the north and east. Or it could be tilted just so as to have the same component in all three directions—up, north, and east. Any and all angles are possible.

QUANTUM SPIN

The first strange difference between the quantum spin of an electron, say, and a real-world gyroscope is that whatever angle we choose to measure for the spinning electron, we will find it either aligned or anti-aligned (opposite direction) with the direction we choose. Let's say we choose to measure in the up direction. Every electron we measure will then spin either aligned with the up direction or the down direction. We will never find an electron only partially aligned with whatever direction we choose to measure. If we measure east, the electron will either be aligned east or west, with no angling toward up or north.

This is very strange, but even stranger is the fact that if we arrange to have a pair of electrons, call them A and B, emitted in such a way that they race off in opposite directions with opposite spins, if we measure electron A to have spin in the up-direction, then electron B will have spin in the down-direction. What is so mysterious about that? It's mysterious because we can arrange the experiment in such a way that the direction we choose to measure is not determined until *after* the pair of electrons is created and each goes racing off in the direction opposite from the other. So we ask:

1. How did electron A know it would have to be aligned either in the up or down direction? Or in the east-west direction if that was our measurement choice? Those are arbitrary directions we choose *after* the electron is already created.

2. How did electron B then know which direction A would find itself forced to choose, thereby forcing B to make the exact opposite choice?

This is still not the pinnacle of strangeness, however. Assume we have created the A and B pair and we have chosen to measure whether the spin of A lies along the north direction. We find that it does. Now from the fact that these are equal and opposite pairs we know that B then has to lie along the south direction. But to be contrary, we choose to make a measurement, and the direction we choose to measure is east, not south. Amazingly there is a 50 percent chance that B lies along the east direction even though from our previous logic we have inferred that, based upon the measurement of A, it must lie along the south direction. The two possibilities are mutually exclusive. Indeed, had we measured B along the south direction we would have found that to be the spin alignment with 100-percent certainty.

This strangeness is telling us that measurement can result in outcomes that contradict the existence of fixed innate properties. The previous example shows this. Electron pair A and B are created in such a way that they must have oppositely aligned spins, and indeed if we measure A to be spinning in the up direction, then if we measure the spin of B in the down direction we are 100-percent guaranteed that it will indeed be spinning in the down direction. But if we were to make a different measurement instead, say measuring whether B is spinning in the east direction, that outcome is possible even though it contradicts a well-inferred property.

There is a contradiction between the predicted outcome of a measurement based upon logic and the actual measurement. If A spins up, B must spin down...and it does if you measure B along that direction. In that case logic and measurement agree. But if you measure along a different direction then B can sometimes be found to spin in that direction even though logic forbids it. Reality appears to be pretty fluid and changeable, as such real experiments show.

BELL'S INEQUALITY

Things remained in this unresolved state of affairs for over a decade. In 1964 John Bell, an Irish physicist working at the European Center for Nuclear Research (CERN, Conseil Européen pour la Recherche Nucléaire) took a year sabbatical in the United States working at Stanford, Brandeis, and the University of Wisconsin in Madison. It was a year well spent: he wound up writing a paper entitled "On the Einstein-Podolsky-Rosen Paradox." In it he proposed yet another variation on EPR, but this time one that could be tested.

What Bell did was to use this difference between the outcome predicted by logic and the outcome resulting from quantum measurements to formulate a series of inequalities based on statistics. For example, if you create millions or billions of electron pairs and you measure A along direction x and B along direction y for some pairs; and A along direction y and B along direction z for some pairs; the total should be greater than A along direction x and B along direction z. This should be true for any angles between the directions. They don't have to be perpendicular. Or to put it in simpler terms, the sum of any two sets of measurements should always be greater than the third set.

As it turns out, for some angles it is...and for some angles it isn't.

That is what was found at last in 1982 by French physicist Alain Aspect. He used photon pairs in place of particle pairs and measured the equivalent of spin, polarization. The Bell inequality turned out to be violated for some angles.

LOCALITY, REALISM, AND THE LEGGETT FORMULA

The Bell inequality is based upon two concepts: locality and realism. Locality means that particles cannot communicate somehow with each other faster than the speed of light. So, if I measure the spin to be up for particle A, there is no way for particle A to communicate this measurement to particle B in time to influence its measurement if they are separated by more than the light travel time. Locality limits the communication of the particles to a "local region" determined by the speed of light.

The second assumption leading to the Bell inequality is realism, meaning that the properties of particles are real, independent of our measurement. The experiment by Aspect showed that nature does not abide by the Bell inequality. Therefore either locality or realism is wrong.

If particles can somehow tell each other instantaneously what measurement is being made on A so that B will then immediately take on the right value, that would be amazing, and violate special relativity. *But an even more astonishing possibility is that the spin, or other quantum properties, do not actually exist until a measurement is made.* The violation of the Bell inequality could be attributed to either one.

In 2003, physicist Anthony Leggett at the University of Illinois, Urbana-Champaign, published a formula that involved making an additional measurement of polarization on pairs of photons, as in the experiment by Aspect. The detection rates found by Aspelmeyer and Zeilinger can be explained only if the quantum theory is correct in the sense that the measurement creates the reality. By making an additional measurement, Aspelmeyer and Zeilinger showed that "reality does not exist when we are not observing it."

"Esse est percipi" (to be is to be perceived) was written by philosopher Bishop George Berkeley nearly three hundred years ago. Consciousness creates reality.

In 1932, mathematician John von Neumann suggested that consciousness-created reality is the inevitable outcome of quantum theory. Nobel Laureate Eugene Wigner concluded from his own arguments about symmetry in physics that the action of matter upon mind must give rise to, as he put it, a "direct action of mind upon matter."

Werner Heisenberg wrote:

Some physicists would prefer to come back to the idea of an objective real world whose smallest parts exist objectively in the same sense as stones or trees exist independently of whether we observe them. This however is impossible. (quoted in The Non-Local Universe: The New Physics and Matters of the Mind, *R. Nadeau and M. Kafatos, eds.)*

In 1979, quantum expert Bernard d'Espagnat stated in *Scientific American*:

The doctrine that the world is made up of objects whose existence is independent of human consciousness turns out to be in conflict with quantum mechanics and with facts established by experiment.

The experiments of Aspelmeyer and Zeilinger have now provided the best evidence yet that this is indeed the case: *consciousness creates reality.*

9

THE POST-PHYSICS ERA

On the day Nicolaus Copernicus died, May 24, 1543, his history-changing book, *De Revolutionibus Orbium Coelestium* (On the Revolutions of the Celestial Spheres) was published. His proposal that the Sun, not the Earth, was at the center of the known Universe—the Solar System more or less in current terms, plus a canopy of stars, whatever they were—is viewed today as the starting point of modern astronomy. This heliocentric (sun-centered) proposal was a pivotal moment in the start of the scientific revolution, but that is only true in retrospect. It was

169

certainly not evident at the time. (And to be fair, the helio-centric view was originally proposed by Aristarchus around 250 BC.)

The prevailing 16th-century geocentric system—that the Sun, the Moon, the planets, and the stars go around the Earth—goes by the name Ptolemaic astronomy, after the great second-century Greek mathematician, geographer, astronomer (and astrologer) Claudius Ptolemaeus—or just Ptolemy in English—who lived in Alexandria. Ptolemy wrote a treatise on astronomy called the *Almagest* that contained, among other things, a star catalog and tables for computing the positions of the five known planets (Mercury, Venus, Mars, Jupiter, and Saturn). This remained an authoritative text and calculational tool at the time of Copernicus.

Since the geocentric Ptolemaeic system was based, as we know today, on erroneous premises, geometrical models for the motions of the planets had to be made more and more complex and elaborate. Imagine off-center wheels upon wheels rotating at rates that were constant only as viewed from an off-center location. The Ptolemaic universe was quite a Rube Goldberg contraption, but owing to all the tweaks and convolutions, the predictions of where the planets would appear in the sky in relation to the stars worked pretty well.

The heliocentric Copernican system was essentially correct…but not 100 percent. The Earth and the other planets in the solar system go around the Sun in orbits that are almost, but not quite, circular. The real orbits are elliptical, but to such a minor extent that if you plot them on a sheet of paper, to the naked eye of all but a keen-eyed, nit-picky draftsman they are indistinguishable from circles. Copernicus also assumed that the motions of the planets on their orbits did not change with position, whereas in fact, as Johannes Kepler discovered, the motions of the planets in their orbits depend on distance to the Sun, which changes for an ellipti-cal orbit.

Because of such limitations, Ptolemy's complex con-trived system was still about as accurate as Copernicus as far as predicting the positions of the planets in the night sky. This goes to show that sometimes faith in the correctness of a system (Copernicus) should trump evidence.

It was many decades before the next critical discover-ies were made. In the years 1609–1610, Johannes Kepler discovered the three key laws of planetary motion, one of which was that the orbits of the planets are elliptical. These came at the very same time as Galileo Galilei's first glimpse of Jupiter and its four major moons which occurred in January 1610. Galileo quickly saw that the system of moons going around Jupiter seemed like a perfect analog of planets go-ing around the Sun.

In many ways astronomy beginning with Copernicus can claim to be the jumping-off point to a new way of thinking about the world and the Universe. But it is the coming of physics, created almost single-handedly by Isaac Newton in his *Principia* (1687), that has been the prime shaper of what we believe in and revere today as the rational, logical scien-tific method. Newton's physics uncovered laws of mechanics and gravity that explained planetary orbits. It became the exemplar of truth and how to achieve it. Physics became the epitome of science, a position it holds to this day.

Physicist David Darling has written in his *Soul Search*:

As a society, we have made the mistake of thinking that because science can answer some questions very well, it might eventually be able to answer all questions. Scientists used to be quite modest in their claims. But recently a number of them have been growing more ambitious, as if the illusory power we have handed them has affected their judgment. The result has been a number of grandiose claims that can be neither justified nor fulfilled. For example, Steven Hawking ended his book A Brief History of Time *with the statement that if this theory about the nature of the universe was upheld, it would help us "know the mind of God." Hawking may be a genius, but his opinions about God carry no more weight than those of his next-door neighbor.... In approaching issues such as death and the afterlife, an open mind and tolerance for all viewpoints are essential. We need to look through the eyes of the scientist and of the mystic and learn what we can from both. In doing this, we shall simply be following the lead of some of the world's truly great thinkers.*

Because of its great successes, amply validated by the attendant technology, physics has acquired such a claim of monopoly on truth at the fundamental level, that when you hear "science" what that generally means is "physics." Physics is taken as the very model of science. For reasons like that the social sciences have often been accused of having physics envy. Indeed, there are social scientists seeking to make their own field more "scientific" by emulating physics. But the pinnacle position of physics as *numero uno* is changing.

THE END OF THE PHYSICS AGE

For the past 300 years physics has claimed to be both the root of all the other sciences and the exemplar of what science should be. Chemistry, for example, is sometimes half-jokingly called "dirty physics" because it deals with the untidy consequences of complex, hence "messy," physics: big molecules, crystals, and the like composed of lots of atoms. It is said that if we knew the laws and particles of physics with absolute precision, we could predict everything known in chemistry. And with a mixture of logic and hubris, perhaps slanted more to the latter, extend that to biochemistry and molecular biology as well so that we could even predict exactly how a strand of DNA serves to organize living things, all based upon the laws of physics. At least that is the way things look "in principle" to many physicists.

But physics today is hitting a brick wall.

By about 1980, physics had had a brilliant run of discovery lasting three centuries back to great Newton. At that time, the standard model of elementary particle physics was quite fully developed. On a single chart, physicists were able to specify which particles appeared to be truly fundamental, such as the electron and neutrino; which particles were composites and what they were composites of, such as the proton and neutron comprised of quarks; and what held such basic but composite particles together: gluons. As physicist Lee Smolin writes in his *The Trouble With Physics*: "For the first time in the history of fundamental physics, theory had caught up with experiment." It was a heady time for physics.

The year before, Smolin had earned his PhD in theoretical physics from Harvard. With such a prestigious degree in hand and a brilliant mind, things must have looked terrific for a career in physics. But in his *The Trouble With Physics,* Smolin, now a world-renowned theoretician in quantum gravity and string theory, laments that when he meets old friends from his graduate days and they ask each other "What have we discovered that our generation can be proud of?" the answer is "Nothing!" Apart from two ex-perimental discoveries—that neutrinos have mass and the existence of dark energy accelerating the Universe (both in-ferred from indirect measurement)—"no new particle has been discovered, no new force found, no new phenomenon encountered that was not known twenty-five years ago" ac-cording to Smolin.

Is this overly pessimistic? What about the discovery of the top quark in 1995? In the sense that Smolin meant, that was more a relief than a discovery. There were good rea-sons to believe that quarks came in pairs in three "genera-tions" with the whimsical names of up and down, strange and charm, bottom and top. In that list they are arranged by mass, which correlates with the energy necessary to detect them in huge particle colliders. With the first five already in the bag via experiments, and pushing to higher and higher energies, is it really a discovery to finally shoot and bag the top quark? In fact, it would have been a far greater discov-ery to find that the theoretically necessary top quark did *not* exist. That would have led physics in a new direction. But the top quark is now in the bag. Now what?

The widely regarded forefront research area of physics is string theory. This is the great hope for going to a far deeper level of understanding. But when the *New York Times* posed the question "What do you believe is true even though you cannot prove it?" to 14 prominent scientists in 2000, physi-cist and Nobel Laureate Philip Anderson painted a gloomy picture of string theory.

Is string theory a futile exercise as physics, as I believe it to be? It is an interesting mathematical specialty and has produced and will produce mathematics useful in other contexts, but it seems no more vital as mathematics than other areas of very abstract or specialized math, and doesn't on that basis justify the incredible amount of effort expended on it.

My belief is based on the fact that string theory is the first science in hundreds of years to be pursued in pre-Baconian fashion, without any adequate experimental guidance. It proposes that Nature is the way we would like it to be rather than the way we see it to be; and it is improbable that Nature thinks the same way we do.

The sad thing is that, as several young would-be theorists have explained to me, it is so highly developed that it is a full-time job just to keep up with it. That means that other avenues are not being explored by the bright, imaginative young people, and that alternative career paths are blocked.

Today physics is in a deep, deep slump. Thousands of papers are written every year on string theory, and yet there is still not one serious experimental test that might show that strings actually exist. The big experimental hope for the new European-based super particle collider, called the Large Hadron Collider, back online following the 2008 accident and shutdown, is to detect the Higgs particle, which in the standard model is supposed to endow particles with mass. Even discovery of the Higgs, sought since the 1960s, would be a mixed success because the Higgs particle would not explain how quarks create the masses of the proton and the neutron (since quarks are governed by the strong force which the theoretical Higgs particle is insensitive to). So yes, there is considerable trouble in Physics City!

THE POST-PHYSICS AGE

Henry Bauer, a chemistry professor and retired dean of arts and sciences at Virginia Polytechnic Institute and State University, has written many articles and books on the philosophy, practice, and politics of science. He now asks the question: if the age of physics as the exemplar of science is coming to an end, what is going to replace it? Or put another way, if in the 20th century the word science almost automatically brought to mind physics, what branch of science will routinely come to mind in the 21st century.

The answer is biology. This has deep implications that spill over into areas beyond science. It will affect our perception of what science is supposed to be. He writes:

As biology becomes the most prominent among the sciences, the conception of what it means to be 'scientific' will also change.

The predominance of biology is evident even looking at the job advertisements of Craigslist. Science jobs are listed solely under "biotech/science," and in fact practically all the listings are for biotech. Bauer's assessment of the situation is right on. Biology is everywhere.

Physics has been successful because it deals with simple, inanimate things for which it is relatively easy to construct and test hypotheses and theories. Its success and resulting prestige have led to the assumption—not limited to physicists themselves, but certainly almost unanimous among them—that simple inanimate things are where the ultimate truth is to be found. But a gene is vastly more complex than an atom.

As systems become more complex, emergent properties come forth. That much is pretty well taken for granted. *But it may also be the case that more complex systems are manifesting innate laws that govern at that level rather than emerge in some collective fashion from simpler states. To put it plainly, there may be laws at work that are not reducible to physics as we know it.*

From the 20th-century view of science as physics, that is pure heresy. From the 21st-century view of science as biology this may become inescapable fact. What is at stake here is the belief in reductionism—understanding something by breaking it apart and examining the behavior of the pieces—as the required tool for the acquisition of verifiable knowledge.

The scientific method itself is sure to undergo a metamorphosis. Proposing hypotheses, conceiving tests that can verify or refute the hypothesis, and then carrying out carefully controlled tests is possible in physics. Such simplicity is not possible in biology. No two creatures of the same species are exactly identical as are two electrons. Case studies, anecdotal reports, histories, and the like will be necessary and accepted approaches to uncovering a very complicated "truth" or at least a truth-for-the-time-being. As is obvious in medical science, you cannot subject a human subject to the equivalent of a particle collider in order to test your hypothesis.

Even such a seemingly indispensible requirement as repeatability will have to yield. Bauer recounts a discussion with a biology friend who had made a major discovery in the field involving strains of yeast. He was aghast when his experiment appeared to not be repeatable at another university. As Bauer reports:

"After months of nerve-wracking mental and laboratory efforts, it was realized that the yeast had mutated as it was moved from one university to another."

Electrons do not mutate.

THE ISSUE OF CONSCIOUSNESS

As biology takes center stage the issue of consciousness will be an ever present one. What is consciousness? Is consciousness a thing separable from matter whose presence is what differentiates the animate from the inanimate? Such a question cannot even be legitimately formulated from the view of physics. Yet I predict it will become a central issue in biology.

Bauer concludes:

Physics-like science sought to explain the cosmos in objective, impersonal terms, formulas and equations. Its goal was and remains an abstract, God's-eye view of universe and man. Its unwarranted hubris has alienated a wide swath of the public. But what we have called 'modern science,' and have regarded as almost a final culmination of millenia of development, is really just adolescent science: brash, contemptuous of older traditions, all too sure of itself, with glib, dogmatic opinions and definite answers. The biology-like science of the future, by contrast, with the mind-body question as a central focus, will have to take a humbler, more realistic, human-scale view of the cosmos— the only view, after all, that humans should aspire to. At the same time, values and meaning will be seen to inhere in the world, a marked and welcome contrast to the science-as-physics view.... ("Science Past, Present and Future," J. Scientific Exploration, Vol. 21, 2007)

At issue is whether it is possible to explain everything in terms of physics *in principle*. I would guess that most people have a feeling that there are areas that physics does a fine job of explaining but others, especially those having to do with human nature, where physics has nothing significant to offer, and is indeed not even relevant. But the question is, will the decline of physics and the ascendance of biology cause scientists themselves to question their assumptions about what reality is? Does it consist solely of particles and force fields, or is there "real reality" beyond the current domain of physics? Are there phenomena that have no bottom-up explanation, even things, like consciousness, that may be far more important ultimately than the discoveries of atom smashers? Can science expand its mindset and its methods rather than try to reduce the phenomena to shoehorn them into the available physics?

10

THE
PRIMACY OF
CONSCIOUSNESS

The origin of the Universe through an act of consciousness is a root belief of all major religions. As religious scholar Prof. Seyyed Hossein Nasr of George Washington University writes in *Mind Before Matter*:

When we turn to the sacred scriptures of various religions, we discover that in every case the origin of the cosmos and of man is identified as a Reality which is conscious and in fact constitutes consciousness understood on the highest level as Absolute Consciousness, which is

181

transcendent and yet the source of all consciousness in the cosmic realm including our own.

Since our cosmos is a realm of matter, consisting of particles and forces acting on particles, the view expressed by Nasr is that consciousness has primacy over matter. It asserts that it was consciousness that created matter, or perhaps even more provocatively that consciousness is continually creating and sustaining the world of matter. I would argue that the evidence from quantum mechanics is actually more supportive of the latter.

This view of the primacy of consciousness prevailed even outside organized religions, as expressed by both Oriental and traditional Western philosophers, according to Nasr. A conscious universe was the all-pervasive worldview throughout much of history, keeping in mind that the "universe" was a far smaller concept for all those centuries than the vast universe of astrophysics today.

ARE YOU NOTHING BUT A PACK OF NEURONS?

The Scientific Revolution beginning in the 17th-century changed this. It brought with it a materialistic, reductionistic philosophy that inert matter is the basis of everything that is real. That view is called "realism" today (in contrast to "idealism" that the world we perceive is not all there is). In the view of realism consciousness is merely a byproduct of brain chemistry, nothing more. Matter, and forces acting on matter, are all there is. This is concisely expressed by Francis Crick in his *The Astonishing Hypothesis: Scientific Search for the Soul,* in which he writes:

You, your joys and sorrows, your memories and your ambitions, your sense of personal identity and free will, are in fact no more than the behavior of a vast assembly of nerve cells and their associated molecules.... You are nothing but a pack of neurons.

Oddly enough, one often gets the impression that those loudly espousing this view, such as Richard Dawkins, derive astonishing glee from such gloom.

Contrast this with the belief of Donald Hoffman, a philosophy professor in the Department of Cognitive Science at the University of California at Irvine, who was among a group of prominent scientists—including Dawkins—to whom the *New York Times* posed the question: "What do you believe is true even though you cannot prove it?" His reply, in part, was:

I believe that consciousness and its contents are all that exists. Space-time, matter and fields never were the fundamental denizens of the universe but have always been, from their beginning, among the humbler contents of consciousness, dependent on it for their very being.

The world of our daily experience—the world of tables, chairs, stars and people, with their attendant shapes, smells, feels and sounds—is a species-specific user interface to a realm far more complex, a realm whose essential character is conscious. It is unlikely that the contents of our interface in any way resemble that realm.

If this is right, if consciousness is fundamental, then we should not be surprised that, despite centuries of effort by the most brilliant of minds, there is as yet no physicalist theory of consciousness, no theory that explains how mindless matter or energy or fields could be, or cause, conscious experience.

This, of course, is quite at odds with the worldview of mainstream science today where the thinking goes: thank goodness, we have long since left behind superstitious pre-modern nonsense. And along with discarding the philosophy of consciousness as a creative basis for the Universe, the philosophy of reductionist materialism has also had to reject any possibility of purpose for the Universe—us included.

QUANTUM MECHANICS REQUIRES CONSCIOUSNESS

Unfortunately for that view, and fortunately for the view that there is indeed a purpose for the Universe, there is the fact that quantum mechanics *requires* consciousness, a point which mathematician John von Neumann made already in 1932 in his *The Mathematical Foundations of Quantum Mechanics* as discussed by Rosenblum and Kuttner:

Von Neumann showed that no physical system obeying the laws of physics (i.e., quantum theory) could collapse a superposition state wavefunction to yield a particular result.... Von Neumann concluded that only a conscious observer doing something that is not encompassed by physics can collapse a wavefunction. Only a conscious observer can actually make an observation.

And as Rosenblum and Kuttner keep hammering on: "Quantum mechanics applies to everything." A one-ton gravitational wave detector must be analyzed using quantum mechanics. They also point out that one-third of our economy is based on products utilizing quantum mechanics, such as lasers and microchips.

Being an astrophysicist, I admit that I myself chafe when I hear vague and scientifically uninformed allusions to the Universe itself somehow being conscious. Remember that it is about 25 trillion miles from here to the nearest star beyond the solar system. There is a lot of empty space out there! The Sun and other stars are huge million-mile in diameter balls of gas with temperatures of around 25 million degrees Fahrenheit at their cores, where the gas is many times denser than lead. What better description than inert hell for a condition like that?

I do find it difficult to leap from the abstract concept of a conscious Universe to one that involves the "real" Universe with all its vast expanses and evidently inert matter. But if consciousness is behind the Big Bang, then it is ultimately the foundation of everything, regardless of the limits of my ability to picture this.

Freeman Dyson, a world-renowned expert on quantum mechanics, solid-state physics, and nuclear engineering, and winner of the Lorentz medal and the Planck medal, had this to say about consciousness and the Universe.

It would not be surprising if it should turn out that the origin and destiny of the energy in the universe cannot be completely understood in isolation from the phenomena of life and consciousness.... It is conceivable...that life may have a larger role to play than we have imagined. Life may have succeeded against all odds in molding the universe to its purposes. And the design of the inanimate universe may not be as detached from the potentialities of life and intelligence as scientists of the twentieth century have tended to suppose. (quoted in The Quantum Enigma)

Although still not taken seriously by mainstream science, the notion that consciousness is primary and that this supports the idea that there is an intelligence behind the Universe—hence a purpose for the Universe—does appear to be rising in Western culture. A feeling that a fundamental shift in human consciousness is starting to happen is in the air outside the halls of academia.

SHIFTING CONSCIOUSNESS

Already in the 1980s the late Willis Harman, futurist, Stanford professor, member of the Board of Regents of the University of Calfornia and president of the Institute of Noetic Sciences, wrote in his book *Global Mind Change*:

We are living through one of the most fundamental shifts in history—a change in the belief structure of Western society. No economic, political, or military power can compare with the power of a change of mind. By deliberately changing their images of reality, people are changing the world.

He saw a convergence of science and religion, but one that would change both science and religion. On the religion side he saw a situation of many religions giving way to a single spirituality in which God is no longer separate and

outside us. He saw us discovering the divine nature of ourselves as espoused in the Perennial Philosophy.

But it is not all rosy. There is a dark side as well. Zoolo-
gist and paleoanthropologist Hank Wesselman is a scientist
with a foot in two worlds. He earned his undergraduate and
master's degrees in zoology at the University of Colorado
at Boulder, then went on to receive his doctoral degree in
anthropology from the University of California at Berkeley. But having become interested in spiritual traditions of
indigenous people, he spent 30 years researching evolution
in the Great Rift Valley in Africa and has also trained in
shamanism for more than 20 years. He too sees evidence
that widespread and transformational spiritual awakening
is already underway within Western civilization.

*It is no news to anyone that a widespread spiritual
awakening is currently taking place—one that has two
distinct aspects. On one side, we find a resurgence of
religious fundamentalism that embraces a historic view
derived from the Middle Ages—a literalist belief that
proclaims this world to be the kingdom of a remote,
transcendent authoritarian father-God, alternately
wrathful and beneficent…. On the other side and in
opposition to this view, we have the spiritually awak-
ened and expanded perspective of the secular humanists who perceive an omnipresent, immanent Divine
Presence of Creative Force existing within all creation,
one that is benevolent, life enhancing and life sustaining.*
(Mind Before Matter)

A resurgence of fundamentalism has certainly been
evident, with particularly disastrous results in the Islamic

world. But there is plenty of apocalyptic fundamentalism right here within the United States veritably relishing the idea of a worldwide conflagration, a battle between good and evil, as part of the end of days, the tribulation that will herald the second coming. Part of the world scene does look very dangerous.

A THREE-WAY BATTLE OF BELIEFS

When I began writing my first book on this topic, *The God Theory*, I started my draft with the opening lines:

As we enter a new millennium, Western civilization is deeply divided. Two divergent paths, separated by a chasm, stretch into the distance in front of us. Each leads to a different horizon, as far away as the eye can see or the mind imagine. One is the highway of the conquistador, the other the path of the pilgrim. The choice between them appears to be an all-or-nothing one between science and spirit.

In retrospect, things look considerably more problematic today. In the post 9/11 era, it is evident that we are engaged in a three-way tug of war, not just two. It is not only between science and spirit, it is also between a spirituality that recognizes, exercises, and celebrates the divine creativity that is part of human nature because human nature is a version of God incarnate, and a "spirituality" that would have us be warrior-servants in slavish service to an all too human warlord of a God, an irascible, intolerant, even bloodthirsty tyrant deity: a temperamental Genghis Khan hurling lightning bolts down from the sky. Subservience, not creativity would please this type of "God." It is amazing and discouraging that the worst kind of "slay the enemies of the lord" biblical-era injunctions are resulting in murder and mayhem every day in the 21st century...brought to you in high definition television and countless blogs on the Internet.

In his newspaper column, *Foreign Matters*, Stanford University journalism professor Joel Brinkley wrote:

> *If you want to understand why murderous Islamic ex-tremists still pour out of the Middle East, consider a small drama under way in Saudi Arabia right now.*
> *A few weeks ago, one of the nation's most senior re-ligious authorities directed that two reporters for a mainstream Saudi newspaper should be executed for publishing stories suggesting that religions other than Islam are worthy of respect.*

This is not an idle threat to the lives of these two reporters. Saudi Arabia beheaded 151 individuals in 2007. This is usually carried out in public outside a mosque after Friday prayers. An atheistic world without God is far preferable to a world serving this kind of "God Delusion," to borrow from Richard Dawkins. But I think, nonetheless, that there is a path opening up that leads neither to Dawkins nor the Dark Ages.

REASON FOR HOPE

Perhaps given human nature massive changes are in-evitably filled with conflict. The United States did not gain independence from Britain over tea and crumpets. Heads literally rolled as well during the French revolution. The conflicts in the world today are evident enough. There is no need to dwell on them here. Is there evidence for what I will unabashedly call the enlightening of mankind?

The term *cultural creatives* was coined by sociologist Paul Ray and psychologist Sherry Ruth Anderson to describe a large segment of American society whose concerns are more with humanitarian, ecological, and spiritual matters than wealth and consumption. Published as *The Cultural Creatives: How 50 Million People Are Changing the World* it was not a shallow conclusion. It drew upon 13 years of survey studies on over 100,000 Americans, plus more than 100 focus groups and dozens of in-depth interviews. Cultural creatives—amounting in their estimate to 1/4 of the U.S. adult population—did not seem to fit in between the other two segments in society, which they labeled traditional and modern. Attributes of cultural creatives were more orthogonal, at right angles to rather than in between *traditional* and *modern*. They are both more inward-directed, seeking to explore their own nature, and at the same time more socially concerned and likely to take part in worthy causes to better society. There may be another 100 million cultural creatives in Europe. And women outnumber men by about three to two.

Could this be the vanguard of the enlightenment of mankind?

The notion that change is imperative is easily proven. Even if you were to discount the abundant evidence of man-made global climate change, simple arithmetic shows that with finite resources—one planet of limited size—growth cannot go on indefinitely. It is a logical and mathematical impossibility. The only uncertainty is when things will come to a head. When demand of anything exceeds supply, there will be a change in the availability of that thing. Some changes lead to disruption, some to collapse. Unlike any time in the past, mankind is up against genuine global limits and planet-wide impacts. That has never happened before, so today's claim of historical uniqueness is valid, and should not be discounted as just the latest doomsday jeremiad.

Limiting our concern to spiritual matters, we find that even though the term is not widely used, the new spirituality emerging within the cultural creative sector is in essence the Perennial Philosophy. This fits right in with non-spiritual global issues because the Perennial Philosophy is drawn from most all the world's best core teachings. The distinguishing feature of the new spirituality is that it needs no mediator between God and you: No church, no priest, no guru. We are learning how to connect to God directly, and the key to this is an expanding consciousness. These are to me encouraging signs.

In his recent book, *The Post American World*, Newsweek commentator Fareed Zakaria discusses some interesting contradictions. He first points to a poll showing that 81 percent of Americans think that the United States is on the wrong track, by far the most negative poll in 25 years. Neither the poll nor the book concern themselves with spiritual matters, but the level of anxiety and pessimism appear to Zakaria to go beyond unemployment, foreclosures, and terrorist threats.

Call it existential fear, call it a spiritual void. He writes:

American anxiety springs from something much deeper, a sense that large and disruptive forces are coursing through the world.

So this confirms the obvious: We are living in dark and dangerous times. Correct?

Actually the answer is "not exactly." As Zakaria points out, a University of Maryland team of scholars which has actually looked deeply into the facts finds that "wars of all kinds have been declining since the mid-1980s and that we are now at the lowest level of global violence since the 1950s." The data indicate that the present time may be one of the most peaceful in recorded history.

Such a startling conclusion seems absurd. But two factors are at play. There are many more of us on the planet. More incidents of violence overall may still be consistent with a safer environment for the average human. A bigger factor is the level of global information available, often in real time. The "bandwidth" for news is way beyond the limitations of a handful of television channels broadcasting an hour or so of news every day. Most of what we hear about today would never have made it onto Walter Cronkite's news hour. There was no time for it all.

I do remember the horrors of Vietnam and Cambodia. Two million people died there in the 1970s and that was covered in newspapers and on television. But I heard little about civil wars in Africa in the 1990s that also killed millions.

Mark Twain, of course, famously said that there are "lies, damned lies and statistics." Nevertheless, in terms of numbers things are better than they seem. A transformational spirituality does seem to be emerging between atheism and fundamentalism. The most important feature of this transformational spirituality is the realization that religious institutions are not necessary to connect with God. That power lies within us. After all, we literally are incarnations of God, so where better to look for contact with God than within ourselves? Our consciousness is ultimately one with God's and that makes it creative. If enough of us activate our creative consciousness in a positive way, we can create "A New Earth" as Eckhart Tolle proposes.

11

WHERE DO THINGS STAND?

The question is often posed: Can science and religion coexist with mutual respect and recognition of each other's validity? Is it reasonable to expect one to answer the *how* of existence, the other the *why*? The biologist Stephen J. Gould had this in mind in his idea of "non-overlapping magisteria," complementary domains of knowledge.

If by religion we mean organized institutional religion, I am skeptical. In fact, I do not think that would be a good idea even if it were possible. Organized religions cannot even come to agreement

193

with each other—at least on the public levels. By simple logic, a lot of religious beliefs and dogmas must therefore be wrong because they flatly contradict each other.

Eckhart Tolle writes in his *A New Earth*:

And so religions, to a large extent, became divisive rather than unifying forces. Instead of bringing about an ending of violence and hatred through a realization of the fundamental oneness of all life, they brought more violence and hatred, more divisions between people as well as between different religions and even within the same religion. They became ideologies, belief systems people could identify with and so use them to enhance their false sense of self. Through them they could make themselves "right" and others "wrong" and thus define their identity through their enemies, the "others," the "nonbelievers" or "wrong believers" who not infrequently they saw themselves justified in killing.

On the other hand, the Perennial Philosophy maintains that there are core beliefs, in general acquired from mystical experiences across many cultures, which form a coherent spiritual philosophy. If the Perennial Philosophy is essentially correct, then science is going to have to come to terms with it. An integration of scientific and spiritual concepts will of necessity come about eventually, even though that is not yet widely evident in the sciences. Integration will expand rather than dilute the substance of both. The obstacles lie in fundamentalism in both camps, fundamentalism being defined as rigid belief that you have access to the whole truth. This thinking unfortunately can be found in both religions and science. Beware of claims of certainty, whether from preachers or professors.

MULTIVERSE OR CREATOR?

A major new body of evidence has accumulated in the past two decades. We have seen in Chapter 3 how modern discoveries in astrophysics have led to the conclusion that we live in a universe surprisingly finely tuned for the existence and evolution of life. In addition to the 10 key coincidences leading to a "just right" universe, there are around 30 or so other constants—such as the masses of fundamental particles—which may or may not also be critical. We don't know, for example, why the six quarks have a range in mass so that the heaviest is about 60,000 times more massive than the lightest. Are these values also critical to the origin of life? No one knows, but the fine-tuning could be even more extensive than we currently recognize. That is speculation, of course.

But for the fortuitous values of the 10 key properties of the Universe on page 207 the facts are not in dispute. It is an issue in need of an explanation. As George Ellis, a prominent cosmologist and co-author of research articles with Stephen Hawking writes:

What is clear is that life, as we know it, would not be possible if there were very small changes to either physics or the expanding universe that we see around us. There are many aspects of physics, which, if they were different, would prevent any life at all existing…. We are now realizing that the universe is a very extraordinary place, in the sense that it is fine tuned so that life will exist. (The Dialogue: Where It Stands Today and Why It Matters)

Apart from the dead-end explanation that it is just a lucky accident, you have to either invoke statistics or a creator to make sense of this. Naturally, mainstream science favors the argument that our universe can have properties just right for life without that fact implying a creator or anything special...and this is logically possible if there are huge numbers of other different universes we can never observe. With enough hypothetical universes, a "just right" mix of properties becomes statistically inevitable. So if you are willing to believe in the existence of vast numbers of undetectable universes, you can accept that explanation. The numbers required are huge though: Anywhere from one followed by 500 zeroes to perhaps even an infinite number.

Is this reasonable? Is it a reasonable price to pay to avoid an intelligent creator? It's a judgment call. No-nonsense mathematician, writer, and debunker Martin Gardner wrote a column for *Scientific American* for 25 years and was one of the founding members of the arch-skeptic Committee for the Scientific Investigation of Claims of the Paranormal, that is CSICOP. He did not buy the multiverse solution. In his book *Are Universes Thicker Than Blackberries* he writes.

There is not the slightest shred of reliable evidence that there is any universe other than the one we are in. No multiverse theory has so far provided a prediction that can be tested.... Surely the conjecture that there is just one universe and its Creator is infinitely simpler and easier to believe than that there are countless billions upon billions of worlds, constantly increasing in number and created by nobody. I can only marvel at the low state to which today's philosophy of science has fallen.

There is no way to test the multiverse hypothesis. This is ruled out even in principle because with different laws of physics in different universes—the key hypothesis—there is no possibility of any observation. So it is not a scientifically provable theory. Thus belief in a multiverse is a faith, no matter how you dress it up in scientific language and mathematics.

Also as Ellis points out:

The multiverse theory just postpones the problem; the issue of ultimate causality remains…it just pushes the final question back one stage further.

Where did the laws triggering and sustaining a multiverse come from?

CONSCIOUSNESS AND FREE WILL

The Perennial Philosophy is based on the concept that consciousness is what has created the dream-like reality of a world of matter and energy. At the moment mainstream science rejects this concept, seeking to explain—more precisely to "explain away"—consciousness as a byproduct of brain chemistry. Consciousness is assumed to somehow emerge out of matter if matter gets organized to a sufficient level of complexity in a brain. But the fact of the matter is that science does not know what consciousness is.

Most physicists are blissfully unaware that the creation of physical reality by consciousness is already built into quantum physics and has received validation by rigorous and ingenious experiments involving the Bell inequality and now the even more significant Leggett inequality. The Trojan Horse of creative consciousness has already been brought into the Troy of physics.

Consciousness is of course intimately connected with free will. Most people believe that their actions are a result of their own decisions. Our legal system, the law, certainly makes that assumption. If you pull the trigger no jury is going to find you innocent based on the argument that "my atoms conspired to make me do it."

Obviously there are factors that influence what you do. If you grow up in a crime-ridden ghetto, chances are your actions will be negatively influenced by that. That's not the issue. Free will is deciding to lift your arm or scratch your head or read this book and knowing that it was your own free choice. Who could doubt that?

The physics of Newton could. In fact the physics of Newton implied that you have absolutely no free will. The "my atoms conspired to make me do it" defense is precisely what the physics of Newton demanded. To be clear, Newton himself never claimed such a thing, but the logic of Newtonian physics did. In that view everything in the Universe is made of particles, single atoms, and atoms bound together into molecules. The argument goes as follows. At any given instant of time the position and motion of each atom or molecule precisely leads to the position and motion the next instant. Think of the Universe and everything in it (us included) as a giant billiard table. Once the balls are put in motion, the rest is fully predictable from the point of view of Newtonian physics.

Cutting to the chase, the position and motion of every particle on Earth one hundred million years ago when the dinosaurs roamed the planet leads inexorably to what you did this morning after breakfast. In fact, in the materialist reductionist view of consciousness your very thoughts are just electro-chemical actions of atoms and molecules in your brain. Thus not only did your actions result completely from ancient history, in principle all the way back to the Big

Bang, but so did your thoughts. In this view the Universe is a giant machine, or more precisely an ensemble of machines—such as us—mindlessly grinding away with everything from day one forward totally predictable and impossible to alter including our every thought and emotion.

Surely this is the ultimate bleak view of reality and human nature. It can't get any worse than that. But for over two centuries from the time of Newton onward, this was the logical conclusion to be drawn from physics. Now in practice human beings can hold inconsistent contradictory beliefs and still go about their everyday business. So, even people knowledgeable enough about physics to comprehend the gloomy implications of pure Newtonian physics lived day to day lives as if none of this were true. I am unaware of any attempt to ever do away with criminal law on the basis that no one can bear any responsibility for preordained, inescapable actions on their part. The closest one might come to this is the radical behaviorism psychology of B.F. Skinner with his "Operant Conditioning Chamber" to train birds and rodents to get the food pellets.

With the coming of quantum mechanics and with it the intrinsic imprecision of the Heisenberg uncertainty principle the doors of the bleak causal prison were thrown open. It is no longer possible, even in principle, to precisely predict what will happen from one instant to the next. This alone would be sufficient cause for philosophical rejoicing. But we now know from quantum experiments like those measuring the Bell and the Leggett inequalities that somehow it is consciousness that tells matter what to do, not the other way around. It is a total reversal of the Newtonian view. Yes, Newtonian physics is sufficiently precise to guide a spacecraft from launch at Cape Canaveral to touchdown at a specific location on Mars. No quantum mechanics is directly involved, not even relativity theory is really necessary. But Newtonian physics is no longer king at the fundamental level. That clears the way for free will theoretically, and the recent quantum measurements confirm free will experimentally.

Quantum mechanics rather definitively tells us that at that level consciousness creates reality. Our own experience of consciousness is the pinnacle of unmediated direct knowledge. And the mystical experience of those fortunate enough to have had it takes them to a knowledge beyond words that our consciousness is in reality the very same as the consciousness of a universal creative intelligence. And still the diehard reductionist materialists deny it.

In his book *A Mind So Rare* cognitive neuroscientist Merlin Donald parodies this view:

Consciousness is an illusion and we do not exist in any meaningful way. But, they apologize at great length, this daunting fact does not matter. Life will go on as always, meaningless algorithm after meaningless algorithm, and we can all return to our lives as if nothing has happened. This is like telling you your real parents were not the ones you grew to know and love but Jack the Ripper and Elsa, She-Wolf of the SS. But not to worry…. The practical consequences of this deterministic crusade are terrible indeed. There is no sound biological or ideological basis for selfhood, willpower, freedom or responsibility. The notion of the conscious life as a vacuum leaves us with an idea of the self that is arbitrary, relative, and much worse, totally empty because it is not really a conscious self, at least not in any important way.

EVOLUTION

I have argued that evolution of life-forms is not only scientifically well-established, but it is in fact the most logical way for a Creator to achieve his goal of creating experience through life-forms. A Creator capable of cleverly designing a few basic laws of physics in such a way as to permit the tremendous complexity of life to evolve is, to me, more impressive than a Creator who has to tinker around with making creatures—with some striking failures along the way.

Anti-creator evolution enthusiasts often point to the untidy, makeshift, less than optimal aspects of creatures and their habits. They ask: "What kind of bumbling designer made this?" And they would be quite correct in this criticism if life-forms were the *direct* product of a designer. But they are not. The messy process of evolution is a rather impressive demonstration of what the right basic laws underlying the Universe can accomplish. I see no conflict between God and Darwin. In fact they go well together in my view.

It is one thing—and a correct one, I believe—to see physics leading to chemistry leading to biochemistry leading to molecular biology leading to cells resulting in ever more complex life-forms. It is quite another to assume that this same chain leads to the emergence of consciousness. Consciousness is not a material thing like blood and bones. Consciousness is something every human being knows she has at a level that is innate and personal and completely undeniably certain. But amazingly outspoken scientists make claims such as "Consciousness is an illusion and we do not exist in any meaningful sense." (Dennett via George Ellis)

A mechanistic explanation of organisms and bodies is fine, from atoms to molecules to cells to organisms. But for reductionism to be correct—for all causation to be from the bottom up—you would have to believe that somehow your decision to go see Mozart's "Marriage of Figaro" or a Rolling Stones concert can be traced back to the atomic level.

CAN A SMART PERSON BELIEVE IN GOD?

This is the provocative title of a book by Michael Guillen, theoretical physicist and former science correspondent for ABC News (along with numerous other credentials, he actually has a PhD in three disciplines: physics, mathematics and astronomy, from Cornell). His answer is, of course, yes, and naturally I concur.

We have seen that it is well established now that numerous properties of our Universe together constitute a very special ensemble conducive to the origin and evolution of life. The only rational escape from an intelligence behind this fact is by dreaming up the existence of vast numbers of other unseen universes. There is really no further justification for it than that. If that is what you want to believe, fine, but it does make it your faith. And recall Occam's razor: The simplest explanation is most likely to be the correct one. One intelligence versus vast numbers, or even an infinity, of other universes...the God explanation strikes me as simpler.

It is possible that the rejection of God by mainstream scientists has been overstated. An article in *Nature* cited by Guillen showed that about 40 percent of American physical scientists believe in a personal God. And as Guillen correctly points out, there are then surely scientists who believe in a nonpersonal God as well. While the total percentage is about half what it is for the population in general, it is far from a total rejection. The strident atheists who grab the public limelight are not representative of all scientists. And they are not acting scientifically in any event, because they are asserting iron-clad belief in something that cannot be proven: that there is no God. That is certainly a matter of faith.

The issue is what kind of God one believes in, or indeed what kind of God one does not believe in. I recall the story of a scientist visiting Northern Ireland in the 1970s who was confronted by a group demanding to know whether he was Catholic or Protestant. Thankful that the question was easily disposed of, he replied that he was an atheist, whereupon he was asked: "All well and good, sir, but are you a Catholic atheist or a Protestant atheist?"

What kind of God is acceptable to the rational thinker? Walt Whitman famously said:

God is a mean-spirited, pugnacious bully bent on revenge against His children for failing to live up to his impossible standards.

That is a terrible picture of a creator. I certainly do not find fault with non-believers for not believing in absurd ideas about what God was conceived to be in eras long gone…or that should be long gone. I too reject the following gods.

- Any god who hates or is vindictive.
- Any god who is pleased by cruelty or slaughter in his name.
- Any god needing groveling subservience or slavish worship from mortals. (The really great do not need to be constantly told that they are great.)
- Any god who is jealous of other patently silly gods springing from the human imagination.

- Any god who is made of matter. (Then who made the matter?)
- Any god who lives in a heaven somewhere "up there" in our Universe. (Then who or what made the Universe?)

If this sounds irreverent that's as it should be. I believe that a real God delights in irreverence. Perhaps what the world needs is a book of favorite God jokes, not to ridicule God but to laugh with him.

A PURPOSE

There is no doubt that science does a superb job of explaining the workings of nature. But I maintain that the human experience cannot be captured in the same way by science. No scientific experiment can discern good from evil, nor what is beautiful. Writing about the objective investigation of science Schroedinger said:

It gives a lot of factual information, puts all our experience in a magnificently consistent order, but it is ghastly silent about all and sundry that is really near our heart, that really matters to us. It cannot tell us a word about red and blue, bitter and sweet, physical pain and physical delight; it knows nothing of beautiful and ugly, good or bad, God and eternity. Science sometimes pretends to answer questions in these domains, but the answers are very often so silly that we are not inclined to take them seriously. (Nature and the Greeks, *1951)*

Drawn by the appeal of symmetry (which scientists love), I am tempted to write "And on the other hand, there is no doubt that religion has done a superb job of...." But this side is a lot murkier. There are no generally accepted laws and theories by which to understand God, nothing corresponding to the laws of mechanics and electromagnetism or the General Theory of Relativity on the side of religion. Institutional religions disagree with each other. Sometimes, alas, they even hate each other.

The key is not in finding the true religion from the host of pretenders (though clearly some are better than others). The key is to understand our own nature. Remember: "Thou art that." Your essence (Atman or soul or Christ within) is the same as God's. The simple recognition of that opens the door to a spiritual perspective that does not need the trappings and dogmas of organized religion. Our origin and ultimate destiny are straightforward. Like a cup full of water from the ocean, there is no difference between the contents of the cup (us) and the ocean (God). And when this creation comes to an end, the water in the cup is poured back into the ocean. But in the meantime we are on a free will trip living an adventure in physical reality. We even have the freedom to do things that are destructive, although that is not such a good idea and must ultimately be balanced by the workings of karma, which is likely to be unpleasant. And it is somehow part of the creation plan that the water in the cup is altered by the experience, so that when it is poured back even the infinite consciousness that is God is enriched by our experience, which is, of course, really his experience all along, disguised as us.

The evidence for this lies in the mystical experiences of mankind whose insights are captured in the Perennial Philosophy. But the evidence is also inside our own consciousness. The experiencing of reality in a meaningful way requires a certain amount of forgetfulness about what we truly are. For most of us in a given lifetime that forgetfulness is almost complete. Add to that the religious misinterpretations about who we are and what God is, or on the other hand the simplistic "you are nothing but a pack of neurons" explanation, and it becomes very difficult to access the deepest truth within our own consciousness: "Thou art that."

I believe that we live in a purpose-guided Universe governed by the laws of science. There is no conflict between a Universe of matter and forces and a Universe of purpose, because the purpose is what went into the laws. In order for God to let himself experience a part of his potential, he imagined into existence just the right characteristics that a Universe needed to have in order for life to originate and then to evolve into complex beings, such as you and I. His consciousness caused this and it is his consciousness that we share and that is our essence. But the arena in which all this takes place is fully governed by the laws of nature including Darwinian evolution.

Hence there is ample reason to believe in Einstein, Darwin, and God.

The 10 Critical Properties of the Universe

Ratio of the gravitational to the electric (Coulomb) force	Stronger gravity would result in smaller stars with shorter lifetimes and crowded galaxies; weaker would result in far fewer stars.
Strength of the nuclear force powering stars	Ten percent change either way could prevent star formation.
Average density of matter in the Universe	Deviation of one part in a million billion immediately after the Big Bang could change evolution of the Universe.
Ratio of ordinary matter to dark matter	Cannot be radically different for galaxies to form but in principle could have been vastly different.
Not too large strength of dark energy	A minor increase would have blown the Universe into runaway expansion.
Quantum clumpiness in the moments after the Big Bang	Factor of ten either way makes the difference between a Universe of black holes or an almost empty Universe.

Just right conditions for formation of carbon and oxygen	Both are essential to life, but as Fred Hoyle discovered, a lucky energy resonance lets carbon form inside stars, but fortuitously an analogous resonance does not occur for oxygen, otherwise carbon would be destroyed.
Unusual properties of water compared to other liquids	Boiling point is unusually high, hence remains a liquid in critical range for biological structures. Also the unusual property of being less dense when frozen.
Fact that the neutron is slightly heavier than the proton	If it were the other way around the proton would not be stable and there would be no atoms.
Minute imbalance of matter over anti-matter	Why were there 30,000,001 particles of matter for every 30,000,000 particles of anti-matter in the Big Bang? Had here been perfect balance there would be no stable matter.

BIBLIOGRAPHY

Benz, A. *The Future of the Universe: Chance, Chaos, God?* Continuum Intl. Publ. Group, 2002.

Berg, Rav. *Nano: Technology of Mind over Matter.* Los Angles: Kabbalah Publishing, 2008.

Chown, M. *The Quantum Zoo: A Tourist's Guide to the Never-Ending Universe.* Washington, D.C.: Joseph Henry Press, 2006.

———. *The Never-Ending Days of Being Dead: Dispatches from the Front Line of Science.* London: Faber and Faber, 2007.

Dalai Lama. *The Universe in a Single Atom: The Convergence of Science and Spirituality.* New York: Morgan Road Books, 2005.

Davies, P. *The Mind of God: The Scientific Basis for a Rational World.* New York: Touchstone, 1993.

Dawkins, R. *The God Delusion*. New York: Houghton Mifflin, 2006.

Eddington, Sir A.S. *The Nature of the Physical World*. Folcroft Library Editions, 1935.

———. *Science and the Unseen World*. New York: The MacMillan Co., 1929.

Evans, D. *The Eddington Enigma*, Princeton, N.J.: Xlibris Corp., 1998.

Gingerich, O. *God's Universe*. Cambridge, Mass.: Harvard Univ. Press, 2006.

Guillen, Michael. *Can a Smart Person Believe in God?* Nashville, Tenn.: Nelson Books, 2004.

Haisch, Bernard, *The God Theory: Universes, Zero-Point Fields and What's Behind It All*. San Francisco: Red Wheel/Weiser Books, 2006.

Harman, W. *Global Mind Change: The New Age Revolution in the Way We Think*. Warner Books, 1988.

Harris, S. *Letter to a Christian Nation*. New York: Knopf, 2006.

Haught, J.F. *God After Darwin: A Theology of Evolution*. Boulder, Colo.: Westview Press, 2000.

Hawking, S.W. *A Brief History of Time: From the Big Bang to Black Holes*. New York: Bantam Books, 1988.

Heisenberg, W. *Physics and Beyond: Encounters and Conversations*. New York: Harper and Row, 1971.

Hitchins, C. *God is not Great: How Religion Poisons Everything*. New York: Twelve, 2007.

Huxley, A. *The Doors of Perception*. Harper and Bros., 1954.

———. *The Perennial Philosophy*. New York: Harper and Row, 1944.

Jeans, Sir J. *The Mysterious Universe*. Cambridge Univ. Press, 2009.

Maeterlinck, M. *The Great Secret*. New York: Citadel Press, Carol. Publ. Co., 1969.

Matt, D.C. *God and the Big Bang: Discovering Harmony Between Science and Spirituality*. Woodstock, Vt.: Jewish Lights Publishing, 1996.

Miller, K.R. *Finding Darwin's God: A Scientist's Search for Common Ground Between God and Evolution*. New York: Cliff Street Books, Harper Collins, 1999.

Pfeiffer, T., Mack, J., and Devereux, P. *Mind Before Matter: Visions of a new Science of Consciousness*. Washington, DC: O Books, 2007.

Polkinghorne, J. *Quantum Physics and Theology: An Unexpected Kinship*. New Haven, Conn.: Yale Univ. Press, 2007.

Planck, M. *The Universe in the Light of Modern Physics*. G. Allen and Unwin, 1931.

Prothero S. *Religious Literacy: What Every American Needs to Know—and Doesn't*. San Francisco: Harper, 2007.

Radin, D. *The Conscious Universe: The Scientific Truth of Psychic Phenomena*. HarperEdge, 1997.

Rees, M. *Before the Beginning: Our Universe and Others*. Mass.: Perseus Books, 1997.

———. *Just Six Numbers: The Deep Forces That Shape the Universe*. New York: Basic Books, 2000.

Rosenblum, B. and Kuttner, F. *Quantum Enigma: Physics Encounters Consciousness*. Oxford: Oxford Univ. Press, 2006.

Russell, P. *From Science to God: A Physicist's Journey into the Mystery of Consciousnesss*. Novato, Calif.: New World Library, 2002.

Sagan, C. *The Demon-Haunted World: Science as a Candle in the Dark*. New York: Ballantine Books, 1997.

———. *The Varieties of Scientific Experience: A Personal View of the Search for God*. New York: A. Druyan (ed.), Penguin Press, 2006.

Sholem, G. *Kabbalah*. Jerusalem: Keter Publishing House, 1974.

Silk, J. *The Big Bang*. New York: W.H. Freeman and Co., 1980.

Smith, Huston. *The Religions of Man*. New York: Harper and Row, 1986.

Smolin, L. *The Trouble with Physics: The Rise of String Theory, the Fall of a Science, and What Comes Next*. New York: Houghton Mifflin Co., 2006.

Teilhard de Chardin, P. *The Prayer of the Universe*. New York: Harper Perennial, 1958.

———. *Christianity and Evolution*. New York: Harcourt Brace and Co., 1969.

Tolle, Eckhart. *A New Earth: Awakening to your Life's Purpose*. New York: Dutton, 2005.

Treiman, S. *The Odd Quantum*. Princeton, N.J.: Princeton Univ. Press, 1999.

White, M. *Isaac Newton: The Last Sorcerer*. Perseus Books, 1998.

Wilber, K. ed. *Quantum Questions: Mystical Writings of the World's Greatest Physicists*. Boston: Shambhala, 2001.

Woit, Peter. *Not Even Wrong, The Failure of String Theory and the Search for Unity in Physical Law*. New York: Basic Books, 2006.

INDEX

Absolute, the, 142-143
Absolute God, the, 150
acquisition of wealth, the, 92
Alpha Centauri, 75
altered states of
         consciousness, 146
Anderson,
         Philip, 174
         Sherry Ruth, 190
annihilation signatures, 82
anti-
         people, 82
         proton, 81
         quarks, 81

anti-gravity, 78
antimatter, 81-82, 208
Aquinas, Thomas, 106, 144
Arabi, Ibn, 108
Aristarchus, 170
Aspect, Alain, 166-167
Aspelmeyer, Markus, 154,
         167-168
Atman, 105-106, 108,
         114-115, 127, 138, 205
attachment to things,
         undue, 91
average density of the
         Universe, 75

backward-in-time causation, 62
Batten, Alan, 99, 103
Bauer, Henry, 176-178
behaviorism psychology, 199
Bell, John, 154, 166
Bell inequality, the, 28, 65,
    167, 197, 199
Bell's inequality, 166
Berg, Rav, 121
Berkeley, Bishop George, 168
Big Bang, the, 32, 68, 70,
    74-78, 81-82, 84,
    111-112, 123-125, 130,
    141, 150, 185, 198,
    207-208
biology, the predominance
    of, 176
biotech, 176
Bohm, David, 154, 162-163
Brahman, 105-109, 112,
    114-115, 121, 127, 138
Brinkley, Joel, 189
Buddhism, 114
    Mahayana, 142
carbon, 79
causation, 201
Chandrasekhar,
    Subramanyan, 98
clockwork universe, the, 157
Cohen, Andrew, 128
compactified dimensions, 40

complete determinism, 103
consciousness,
    the issue of, 178
    the role of, 48
consciousness-created
    reality, 168
conservation of momentum,
    162
Copernican Principle, the,
    68, 84
Copernicus, Nicolaus,
    169-170
cosmic consciousness
    event, 144
    experience, the, 146-147
cosmology, definition of, 102
Coulomb force, 70-71, 207
creation by subtraction,
    140-141
creation-out-of-nothing
    problem, the, 139
Crick, Francis, 182
critical density, the, 76
Crommelin, Dr. A.C.D., 95
CSICOP, 196
cultural creatives, 190
Cunninghan, Mr. E.T., 96
d'Espagnat, Bernard, 168
Dalai Lama, the, 35-37, 42
dark energy, 77, 207
dark energy accelerating
    the Universe, 174

dark matter, 75-76, 207
dark matter ratio, the, 77
Darling, David, 171
Darwin's evolution, 102
Darwinian evolution, 32, 68, 83-84, 131, 206
Davies, Paul, 81
Dawkins, Richard, 41-42, 87, 109-110, 119, 183
de Broglie, Louis, 56
deification, 122
Democritus, 124
determinism, 157, 159, 162
    complete, 103
Deus Absconditus, 106
deuterium, 73-74, 81
Dominican Order, 113
Donald, Merlin, 200
Druyan, Ann, 37
Dyson,
    Freeman, 185
    Sir Frank, 95-96
Eddington, Sir Arthur, 93, 95-96, 98-104, 114-115
Ein-Sof, 106-107, 121-123
Einstein, 33, 72, 159
Einstein's General Relativity, 98
Einstein's General Theory of Relativity, 93-94

Einsteinian gravity, 94
Einstein-Podolsky-Rosen paradox, the, 166 (*see also* EPR paradox, the)
Ellis, George, 195, 197
EPR, the, 152, 154, 159-163, 166 (*see also* Einstein-Podolsky-Rosen thought experiment)
EPR paradox, the, 163
Euclidean geometry, 93
evolution, 201
    role of, 130
expanding consciousness, an, 191
expansion of the Universe, 77-78, 137
fertility of God, the, 113
first key value setting the stage for life, 71
Franks, Felix, 80
free will, 130, 152, 158-159, 197-198, 200, 205
fundamentalism, 187-188, 192
    definition of, 194
futurity, 149
Galilei, Galileo, 171
Gardner, Martin, 196
General Relativity, 93-94, 98, 104

General Theory of
    Relativity, the, 205
gluons, 173
God
    consciousness, 148
    power, 139
God Theory, The, 68, 134, 139
Godhead, the, 106-108, 113,
    116, 120-123, 128, 137
Gottfried Leibnitz, 89
Gould, Stephen J., 193
gravitational self-attraction
    of matter, 78
gravity and electricity, 70
Guillen, Michael, 202
Harman, Willis, 186
Harris, Sam, 87-88
Hartle, James, 111
Haught, John, 130-131
Hawking, Stephen, 111, 195
Hawking-Hartle view, the, 112
Heinlein, Robert, 142
Heisenberg, Werner, 45,
    124, 132, 156, 168
Heisenberg uncertainty
    principle, the, 152,
    154-161, 199
heliocentric Copernican
    system, the, 170
helium-three, 73
Henry, Richard Conn, 125
Higgs particle, the, 175

Hitchins, Christopher, 87
Hoffman, Donald, 183
Hubble, Edwin, 75
Hubble horizon, the, 75
Huxley,
    Aldous, 90, 92,
    100-101, 134, 142
    T.H., 103
Hyades cluster, the, 96
idealism, realism vs., 182
incommensurable
    quantities, 156
infinite
    conscious
        intelligence, 85
intelligence, 106, 125, 131
inflation fields, 125
intellectual pride, 92
intelligent creator, an, 196
Intelligent Design, 21, 68,
    82, 132
intelligent universes, 43
interference pattern, 55-56
irreducible complexity, 83
Jeans, Sir James, 85,
    102-104, 110
Jordan, Pascual, 49
Judaism, 121
"just right" universe, a, 195
Kaballah, 106, 121, 123, 127
karma, 133, 205
Kepler, Johannes, 170-171

Kuttner, Fred, 48-50, 58, 184-185
Lao Tzu, 137
Large Hadron Collider, 175
laws of quantum mechanics, the, 59
Leggett, Anthony, 154, 167
Leggett inequality, the, 44, 65, 197, 199
Leucippus, 124
life-friendly laws of nature, 123
local realism, definition of, 29
locality, definition of, 167
LSD trips, 146-147
Mahayana Buddhism, 142
Manhattan Project, 162
materialism,
    definition of, 36
    radical scientific, 37
    reductionist, 43, 56, 184
    scientific, 38
materialist reductionist view, the, 198
materialists, reductionist, 124
Matt, Daniel, 127
Matthews, Robert, 80
measurement problem, the, 49
mechanistic view of matter, 103
Meister Eckhart, 113-115, 120, 122-123, 142
Middle East, the, 88
Milky Way Galaxy, 71
minute uncertainties, 156

M-theory, 38, 40-41, 90
multiverse
    hypothesis, the, 197
    solution, the, 196
mystical experience, the, 107, 116, 142
Nasafi, Aziz, 110
Nasr, Seyyed Hossein, 181
near-death experience, 148
new spirituality, the, 191
Newton, Isaac, 171
Newton's physics, 102-103
Newtonian
    gravity, 94
    physics, 159, 198-200
nihilism, 37
non-physical
    realities, 90
    reality, 92, 102
    realms, 41, 123
nuclear force, the, 72
Occam's razor, 202
Omega Point, 132-134
Oppenheimer, Robert, 162
other
    dimensions, 91
    realities, 92
    universes, 41
Pauli, Wolfgang, 132
Perennial Philosophy, the, 16, 89-114, 120, 126, 134, 137, 141, 187, 191, 194, 197, 206

three essential tenets
    of, 90-91
Philo of Alexandria, 110
photons, 55
physics of Newton, the, 198
Plato, 124
Podolsky, Boris, 160
polarity, 150
polarization, 166
poor in spirit, definition of
    being, 91
positron, 81
predominance of biology,
    the, 176
primacy of consciousness,
    182-192
primary cause, a, 110
psychedelics, 147
Ptolemaeus, Claudius, 170
Ptolemaic astronomy, 170
Ptolemy, 170-171
quantum
    clumpiness, 207
    clumps, 78
    fluctuations, 34, 78, 84
    gravity, 173
    laws, 34-35, 84
    mechanics, 44, 48,
        60-61, 66, 90,
        103, 124-125,
        155, 168, 182,
        184-185, 199-200
    mechanics, the laws
        of, 59

physics, 48, 57, 104, 152,
    158, 160, 197
    spin, 164-165
    theory, 163, 168-169
quarks, 174-175, 195
radical scientific
    materialism, 37
random
    universe theory, 85
    universes, 85, 125
ratio of the gravitational
    force to the electric
    force, 71
Ray, Paul, 190
realism vs. idealism, 182
realism, definition of, 167
reductionism, 177, 201
    definition of, 36
reductionist
    materialism, 43, 56, 184
    materialists, 124, 200
reductionists, 132, 134
Rees, Sir Martin, 33, 83
relativity theory, 50
Riemann, Bernhard, 93
role of consciousness, the, 48
Rosen, Nathan, 160
Rosenblum, Bruce, 48-50,
    58, 184-185
Sagan, Carl, 37-38, 83
Sankara, 108
Schopenhauer, Arthur, 113
Schroedinger, Erwin, 90,
    110, 204

Schroedinger's Cat thought experiment, 59-62
scientific materialism, 38
Scientific Revolution, the, 182
scientism, 43
shamanism, 187
Sholem, Gershom, 121
Skinner, B.F., 199
Smith, Dr. Allan, 144, 146-147
Smolin, Lee, 39, 143, 173-174
solid-state physics, 185
spacetime, 93, 137, 143
special and general relativity theories, 33
theories of relativity, Einstein's, 159
special relativity, 167
Special Relativity, 94
spiritual nondualism, 116
St.
Augustine, 112, 144
Bernard of Clairvaux, 126
John of the Cross, 141
stable atom problem, the, 155
Stenger, Vitor, 87
Steuco, Agostino, 89
still small voice, 115
string theory, 33, 38-41, 43, 90, 124-125, 173-175
string-theory universes, 35
supernovae, 78

superposition of states, 61
Susskind, Leonard, 33, 83
Tart, Charles, 146
Teilhard de Chardin,Pierre, 132-134
teleological view of evolution, a, 132
10 key properties of the Universe, the, 195, 207-208
tensor calculus, 99
thought experiment, definition of a, 153
three essential tenets of the Perennial Philosophy, 90-91
timelessness, 144
Tolle, Eckhart, 89, 192, 194
top quark, the, 174
transformational spirituality, 192
ultimate
reality, 100
source, the, 91
uncaused
causes, 125
God, an, 110
undetectable universes, 84, 196
undue attachment to things, 91
universal creative intelligence, a, 200
unseen universes, 202

Vedanta, 105-106, 108
Vedantic
       terms, 113
       texts, 115
Vedral, Vlatko, 154
void, the, 141
von
       Hochheim, Eckhart, 113
       Neumann, John, 168,
       184
Wasselman, Hank, 187
water, 80
wavefunction, the, 57-61
       collapse of, 59
what is real, 158
Wheeler, John Archibald, 62
Wheeler's delayed choice
       experiment, 62
Wigner, Eugene, 168
Wilber, Ken, 128
Woit, Peter, 39-40
Wren-Lewis, John, 148-149
Zakaria, Fareed, 191-192
Zeilinger, Anton, 154,
       167-168
zero-point energy, 80-81

ABOUT THE AUTHOR

Bernard Haisch, PhD, is an astrophysicist and author of more than 130 scientific publications. He served as a scientific editor of the *Astrophysical Journal* for ten years, and was Principal Investigator on several NASA research projects. After earning his PhD from the University of Wisconsin in Madison, Haisch did postdoctoral research at the Joint Institute for Laboratory Astrophysics, University of Colorado at Boulder and the University of Utrecht, the Netherlands. His professional positions include Staff Scientist at the Lockheed Martin

221

Solar and Astrophysics Laboratory; Deputy Director of the Center for Extreme Ultraviolet Astrophysics at the University of California, Berkeley; and Visiting Scientist at the Max-Planck-Institut fuer Extraterrestrische Physik in Garching, Germany. He was also editor-in-chief of the *Journal of Scientific Exploration*. Prior to his career in astrophysics, Haisch attended the Latin School of Indianapolis and the St. Meinrad Seminary as a student for the Catholic priesthood. His first book, *The God Theory*, received excellent reviews. He is married, with three children, and lives in the San Francisco Bay Area with his wife, Marsha Sims.